FOCH

MILITARY PROFILES

SERIES EDITOR
Dennis E. Showalter, Ph.D.
Colorado College

*Instructive summaries for general and expert
readers alike, volumes in the Military Profiles
series are essential treatments of significant and
popular military figures drawn from world history,
ancient times through the present.*

FOCH

Supreme Allied Commander
in the Great War

Michael S. Neiberg

BRASSEY'S, INC.
Washington, D.C.

Library of Congress Cataloging-in-Publication Data

Neiberg, Michael S.
Foch : Supreme Allied Commander in the Great War /
  Michael S. Neiberg.
        p.   cm.—(Military profiles)
      Includes bibliographical references and index.
      ISBN 1-57488-672-X (alk. paper)
      1. Foch, Ferdinand, 1851–1929.   2. Marshals—
  France—Biography.   3. World War, 1914–1918—
  Campaigns—Western Front.   4. Leadership.
  5. Command of troops.   6. World War, 1914–1918—
  Diplomatic history.   I. Title.   II. Series.

  DC342.8.F6N45 2003
  940.4'144'092—dc21   2003013251

Brassey's, Inc.
22841 Quicksilver Drive
Dulles, Virginia 20166

FIRST EDITION

10 9 8 7 6 5 4 3 2 1

Contents

List of Maps

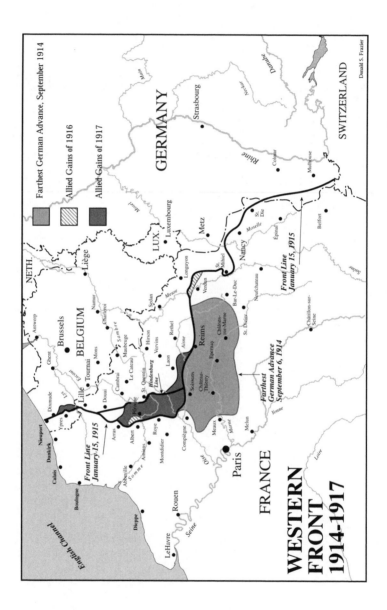

Donald S. Frazier

WESTERN
FRONT
1914-1917

Preface

Across the Seine River from the Eiffel Tower, just behind the Trocadéro, sits a statue of Ferdinand Foch on horseback. The statue faces across the river and the Champ de Mars toward the École Militaire, home of the École Supérieur de Guerre (France's highest professional military school), where Foch first made a name for himself as an instructor of military history, strategy, and applied tactics. Just a short walk away is a beautiful gold-domed building, Les Invalides, where Foch spent his retirement. As it was then, Les Invalides is today the resting place of the tomb of Napoleon and the tombs of several of France's greatest military heroes, including Turenne and Vauban. Upon his death in 1929, Foch was laid to rest in a chapel near that of Napoleon. It stands out from the rest by virtue of its emotional power: Foch's casket is carried on the shoulders of eight French soldiers carved out of black stone. These Parisian monuments, easy for any tourist to visit today, serve as fitting memorials to the greatest French soldier of the twentieth century—a man who shaped the definition and conception of the modern general.

Foch's exceptional career, culminating in his command of the Allied armies in 1918, was in many ways anomalous. Unlike most of the successful generals of his career, he never served in France's overseas colonies. As a result he had no practical experience in warfare. When he led the Twentieth Corps into action in Lorraine in 1914, it was the first time that he had been in combat. Moreover, he, along with his patron Joseph Joffre, was among the small minority of senior French officers in 1914 who were not graduates of the military academy at St. Cyr. He had made his name in the classroom as an advocate of the offensive school of warfare, not on the fields of battle of Madagascar, Morocco, or Indochina.

More remarkably, Foch was one of a small number of generals who were in senior leadership positions in 1914 and 1918. Unlike Helmuth von Moltke, Joseph Joffre, John French, Pavel Rennekampf, and so many other highly regarded prewar generals, Foch played key roles in campaigns at both the start and the end of the war. He did so by taking the unusual step of completely reforming all of his ideas about the nature of war. During the war, he told one interviewer, "I have only one merit. I have forgotten what I taught, and what I learned."[1]

While that insight is revealing of Foch's modest personality, he had many more merits than an ability to forget his own teachings. Even his rivals recognized in him exceptional intelligence, dedicated professionalism, and an ability to make men perform at their very best. Gen. Tasker Bliss, Chief of Staff of the American Army during World War I, noted that Foch had an "unteachable ability to foresee the future—to read his opponent's mind."[2] That ability, while perhaps unteachable, came from Foch's lifelong study of the German military in the hopes that he might find himself in exactly the position he held on July 18, 1918. On that day, German armies advanced so close to Paris that the city's residents could hear their guns. The French government prepared the capital for a siege and planned to evacuate to Bordeaux as it had done in 1914. Foch, who had played a key role in stopping the Germans four years earlier, now had the responsibility of stopping this new German offensive and saving Paris. It was an opportunity that he had prepared for his entire life and it was one he had no intention of wasting.

My thanks to Bill Astore, Dennis Showalter, and Mark Grotelueschen for taking the time to read this manuscript and provide me with excellent feedback. I take full responsibility for all translations, though I must acknowledge the help I received from Nicole Smith, Rich Lemp, and Scot Allen. Still, if any errors remain, they are mine alone. I must also thank my friends Gen. Hugues Silvestre de Sacy and Joëlle de Sacy for their kind hospitality in Paris. General de Sacy and the staffs of the Service Historique de L'Armée de L'Air and of the Service Historique de L'Armée de Terre were kind enough to help with photographs. Thanks are also due to Don Frazier for the maps and to Paul Merzlak for supporting this project from the beginning.

I dedicate this book with love to my wife, Barbara, who first took me to the Trocadéro.

Chronology

1851	Ferdinand Foch born at Tarbes, *October 2.*
1870	Volunteered for service in the Fourth Infantry Division.
1872	Graduated from the École Polytechnique.
1874–85	Assigned to artillery regiments in Tarbes, Saumur, Rennes, and Paris.
1883	Married Julie Bienvenüe.
1885	Enrolled as a student at the École Supérieur de Guerre.
1887	Assigned to Headquarters, Sixteenth Corps, Montpellier.
1890	Assigned to Troisiéme Bureau (Operations) of General Staff, Paris.
1892	Assigned to Thirteenth Artillery Regiment, Vincennes.
1895	Named Professor of Military History, Strategy, and Tactics at the École Supérieur de Guerre.
1901	Sent in "exile" to the Twenty-ninth Artillery Regiment, Laon.
1903	*Principes de la Guerre* published.
1904	*Conduite de la Guerre* published.
1905	Named Chief of Staff of the Fifth Corps, Orléans.
1908	Named commander of the École Supérieur de Guerre.
1909	Paid official visit to British Staff College at Camberely.
1910	Attended military maneuvers in Russia.
1913	Named commander of Twentieth Corps, Nancy.

1914   Deaths of son, Germain, and son-in-law, Charles Bécourt, *August;* French forces defeated at the Battle of Morhange.

French forces won the First Battle of the Marne, *September.*

Ypres and Yser Campaigns began *October.*

1915   Named "Commander of the Armies of the North," *January.*

Assaults on Vimy Ridge failed, *May.*

1916   Somme campaign began, *July.*

1917   Named Chief of Staff of the French Army, *May.*

Coordinated Italian recovery efforts, *October.*

1918   Doullens agreement gave Foch power to coordinate Allied efforts, *March.*

Beauvais agreement extended Foch's authority to direct Allied strategy and counteroffensives, *May.*

Named Marshal of France, *August.*

Armistice signed with Germany, *November 11.*

Elected to the Académie Française, *November.*

1919   Refused to attend signing of the Versailles Treaty, *June.*

Victory march down the Champs Elysées, *July.*

Named Marshal of Great Britian, *August.*

1920   Presided over inauguration of France's tomb of the unknown soldier.

1921   Delivered elegy to Napoleon and toured the United States.

1922   Attended the funeral of Henry Wilson in London.

1923   Toured Eastern Europe and named Marshal of Poland.

1929   Foch died on March 20 in Paris and was placed in Les Invalides.

FOCH

Chapter 1

The Formation of Ferdinand Foch

F ERDINAND FOCH was born in 1851 into the "old France": conservative, devoutly Roman Catholic, and intensely patriotic. Like his future fellow World War I army commanders Edouard-Noël de Castelnau and Joseph Joffre, Foch was from the Pyrenees, a traditional region near the Spanish border far from the political and social turmoil of Paris. Foch's birthplace, Tarbes, is just twelve miles from Lourdes, where, in 1858, many Catholics believed that the Virgin Mary appeared in the Grotto of Massabielle and spoke to a local girl. The region quickly became a location for pilgrims. The "miracle of the grotto" reinforced the faith of many residents of the area, including the Foch family, for whom Catholicism had long been a bedrock. Ferdinand's brother, Germain, joined the Jesuits (a decision that later caused Ferdinand a great deal of unwarranted trouble), and Ferdinand himself remained a devout Catholic his entire life.

The military formed the second important pillar of Foch's early life. Napoleon decorated Foch's maternal grandfather with the Legion of Honor for bravery in fighting in Italy, Spain, and Austerlitz. The Emperor himself wrote, "Here is a brave man" on the accompanying citation. One of Foch's uncles rose from drummer boy to general; he was a frequent subject of family lore. Napoleon became an object of worship in the Foch household and the Foch family admired Napoleon III's Second Empire as a brilliant expression of French pride and accomplishment. Still, Ferdinand's father, aptly named Napoleon, hoped that Ferdinand would instead enter the civil service as he himself had done.

The twin influences of Church and army had exerted their power early over Foch's life. In 1870, while studying at a Catholic school in the eastern French city of Metz, Foch joined the Fourth Infantry Division to help repel German invaders at the onset of the Franco-Prussian War. Once enlisted, the young Foch saw a parade-ground army, filled with officers who looked impressive but lacked the qualities needed to win wars. He also witnessed a French rank and file long on spirit but short on competent leadership. Although he experienced no combat, the disorganization and chaos apparent in the French army of 1870 and 1871 marked him indelibly.

France's defeat in the Franco-Prussian War cost the nation dearly. Germany seized the provinces of Alsace and Lorraine, deeply wounding French pride and removing two vital economic districts. France also paid an indemnity of 1.5 billion francs and agreed to an occupation force of 50,000 German troops until the indemnity was paid in full. France also suffered the double humiliation of a German victory march down the Champs Élysées and the crowning of Kaiser Wilhelm I at Versailles, the traditional seat of French power. Unable to prove his bravery under fire because he saw no combat, the patriotic Foch returned to Metz intent on finishing school so he could become an officer and one day do his part to avenge this mortifying defeat. The national emergency also convinced Foch's parents to support his decision to pursue his calling in the army as his brother was pursuing his own in the Catholic Church.

After the war, Foch returned to Saint Clement's school in Metz where he had to share the city with occupying German forces. Metz was the headquarters of German occupation commander General Edwin von Manteuffel, who ordered German military bands to play martial music regularly to remind the locals of their nation's defeat. In Nancy, Manteuffel ordered the bands to play "Retreat" every day. Foch took his entry exams for the French officer corps while listening to a German military band play martial music, an indignity he never forgot. In 1918, when French armies entered Metz, Foch ordered six regimental bands brought in to play French patriotic music in the streets so that the sounds might be heard in every home in the city.

His anger while taking his exams helped to motivate him, for he did well enough to gain an appointment at the prestigious École Polytechnique in Paris. In 1871, the city made a deep first impression on the young man from the provinces. Parts of the capital, including the Hôtel de Ville (city hall), were still smoking from the battles of the Paris Commune (see below). Communards were still being executed as he arrived to begin his studies. The billiard room at the École Polytechnique was unusable, as it had been converted into a makeshift morgue. The walls remained bloodstained during Foch's entire time there.

Foch's early military assignments after graduation from the École Polytechnique gave him a wide knowledge of France. He chose artillery, Napoleon's arm, and went to the French artillery school at Fontainebleau. After a tour in his hometown of Tarbes, he attended the cavalry school at Saumur in the Loire Valley, then served at Rennes, in the heart of Brittany, before returning to Paris in 1880. Foch was one of the few senior officers of his generation not to serve in the colonies, an important path to promotion for future generals like Joseph Joffre (whom Foch had first met when both were students at the École Polytechnique), Hubert Lyautey, Joseph Galliéni, and others. Because he saw Germany as France's overriding security concern, Foch did not seek overseas assignments. Instead, he served in units across France, giving him a distinct understanding of the country and its people, as well as its strategic liabilities and assets.

While in Brittany, he met and married Julie Bienvenüe, a woman from a devout Breton family. Like Foch, she was intensely patriotic. In 1918, when many Parisians fled the capital in the face of advancing German armies, Julie Foch kept her family in Paris, confident in her husband's promise to her that she was safe because he would stop the German advance before it reached the capital. She was also wealthy, and the marriage made Foch much more financially secure than most of his peers. In 1895, he purchased a château and seventy-acre estate near the Breton town of Morlaix. Foch had a private chapel built for prayer and reflection. Brittany became his home and refuge, but the army remained his, and his family's, primary focus: Foch's son joined the army, and both of his daughters married army officers.

In 1885, Foch received an appointment as a student at the École Supérieur de Guerre, located inside the École Militaire on the Champ de Mars in Paris. It proved to be a turning point in his career and his life. Captain Foch was thoroughly impressed by the quality and energy of the students and instructors he met at the École Supérieur de Guerre. He focused his attention on a detailed study of German society and on a deep and intensive reading of European military manuals. His studies also included heavy doses of the German military philosopher Carl von Clausewitz. He concluded that in a future war with Germany, France would have to find ways to compensate for German superiority in numbers, training, and equipment. The innate superiority and élan of the French soldier, he believed, were the most important advantages that France could count on in the future.

In 1887, Foch graduated fourth in his class from the École Supérieur de Guerre and continued his odyssey across France as a staff officer in the Sixteenth Army Corps at Montpellier in the south. He returned to Paris in 1890 to serve on the Operations Bureau of the General Staff at a time of intense political intrigue. The extremely popular former general Georges Boulanger seemed on the verge of a coup d'état that would overthrow the Third Republic, a government despised by many French officers. Foch wisely avoided public discussions of "The Boulanger Affair," which ended with a warrant for Boulanger's arrest and the general's subsequent exile. Whatever his feelings on the matter, they remained personal.

Foch displayed the same wisdom regarding political silence during the infamous Dreyfus Affair, which began in 1894 and continued off and on until Dreyfus's exoneration in 1906. Dreyfus, an Alsatian, Jewish captain serving on the French general staff, had been unjustly convicted of espionage. As evidence of his innocence came to light, "Dreyfusards" (led by future French prime minister Georges Clemenceau) advocated for a new trial. "Anti-Dreyfusards" believed that a new trial would only weaken the army and national defense. The scandal tore France apart when the army came under intense scrutiny for covering up evidence of Dreyfus's innocence.

The scandal's severity eventually forced most politicians and officers to choose sides. Foch was not immune to the antirepublicanism that plagued conservative France in these years, but he was careful not to involve himself in the politics of the day. The treacherous political environment of the Third Republic was a veritable minefield for officers to tread, as Republicans continued to assail the Catholic Church and reduce its influence. Foch, having a Jesuit brother, was in a particularly exposed position. While it is unlikely that Foch sympathized with Dreyfus or his supporters, he was wise enough to subordinate politics to professionalism.

Foch's silence on political matters fit into a time-honored, but too-seldom-practiced, tradition of French officers removing themselves from domestic politics. The Dreyfus Affair put this practice, known as *La Grande Muette* (Great Silence), into serious jeopardy. Foch believed that, regardless of Dreyfus's actual guilt or innocence, the intellectuals defending Dreyfus were acting unpatriotically by publicly criticizing the army and placing it under a national microscope. Still, he clung to the three fundamental principles of *La Grande Muette*: loyalty to the republic, respect for the government, and obedience to the law. Like all French soldiers, Foch was forbidden by the constitution of the Third Republic from voting. Some officers chose other, more public, outlets for their political views; by contrast, Foch followed the tradition of *La Grande Muette* so carefully that his wife's political views during this period are better understood today than are his own.

Foch's personal contacts reveal that his first allegiance was always to the army and the nation, not to any political or religious subgroup within the army. Although he was a graduate of the École Polytechnique, not the French military academy at St. Cyr, he was nonetheless well connected within the elite of the French army. His closest associates were the republican Joseph Joffre, who famously demanded to eat meat on Fridays to prove that he was not a practicing Catholic, and Charles Millet, one of the French army's few senior Protestant generals. On the other hand, Foch did not have close relationships with several prominent Catholics, including Edouard-Noël de Castelnau, who was a lay member of the Capuchin order and nicknamed "The Fighting Friar." It is likely that Foch disapproved of Castelnau's unwillingness to separate his profession and his faith. Foch's allegiance to the army as a band of brothers in service to France made later allegations of pro-Catholic and antirepublican bias sting him all the more.

The deepest roots of the Third Republic's internecine political crises lay in the memories of the Franco-Prussian War and the Paris Commune. To most members of conservative France, including Foch, the Commune had been an illegitimate experiment in left-wing mob politics. The Commune's destruction in the "bloody week" of May 21–28, 1871, had been grim, but necessary to stop a new reign of terror. To the Left, however, the enthusiasm with which the army put down the Commune conflicted sharply with the poor performance it had displayed against Prussia the previous fall and winter. Even as the French regular army was engaged in crushing the Commune, the occupying Prussian army that it had failed to defeat stood at the gates of the city watching as the French engaged in civil war.

Political instability led to military instability. France had forty-two war ministers between 1871 and 1914. In 1898 alone, five war ministers had been in office. Henri Bergé, a friend of Foch and a long-time member of the Supreme War Council, expressed his frustration in a letter to Foch thus: "I am to see the new war minister Wednesday. This will be my forty-sixth. I want to see how this one differs from the previous forty-five."[1] As each new broom swept the ministry clean, important jobs changed hands and made continuity at senior levels very difficult. Some generals, like the avowedly prorepublican Maurice Sarrail, learned to play the political system well and got promoted quickly. Political intrigue ran against Foch's nature; he developed an intense dislike for politicians of all ideologies. Despite a less distinguished military record, Sarrail was promoted to colonel three years ahead of Foch.

Notwithstanding the poisoned environment of Parisian politics, Foch returned to the École Supérieur de Guerre in 1895 as an assistant professor. There he began the teachings that made him so well known in military circles. Foch still clung to the belief that Germany was materially superior to France. Thus he lectured to his students about the "sovereign virtues of the will to conquer" and the need to have absolute faith in the offensive. An overreliance on the defensive, he argued, had caused France's defeats in 1870. Because he had never served in the colonies, his focus remained fixed on Germany and the problems of continental warfare, which he saw above all as a supreme test of national wills.

In the classroom, Foch combined the intellect of a studious officer with the proselytizing faith of a priest. One biographer noted that he treated his position as an "educational pulpit of the army" to preach the virtues of faith, the offensive, and the inherent superiority of French national character to German.[2] To Foch, service to France was akin to service to God. His work at the École Supérieur de Guerre took on the personal importance of a sacred duty. The École Supérieur de Guerre was of critical importance to France, Foch believed, because it could provide officers with talent worthy of the energy and patriotism of the French soldier. Foch therefore threw himself body and soul into his work there. Even his rivals and critics admired the infectious spirit with which he spoke of France, and the chance he prayed he would have one day to right the wrongs of 1870 and 1871.

In spite of his passion, patriotism, and careful silences, the politics of France's Third Republic soon caught up with him. In 1899, the civilian war ministry attained the right to name colonels and generals. Foch was a victim of the plan that republican Minister of War Louis André formulated to collect intelligence on the political leanings of all French officers. André used this intelligence to compile a dossier on each officer in the French army. Believing that political reliability was more important than military capability, André oversaw a broad and ambitious program to identify and promote to senior rank only those officers with open republican sympathies. Avowedly Catholic officers were especially suspect.

Foch, whose politics were unknown but whose faith was surely not, sat in a dangerously exposed position. André held up Foch's promotion to colonel for three years and, in 1901, André removed him from his post at the École Supérieur de Guerre. Foch believed that the treatment he had received was a direct result of his having a Jesuit brother. His next two assignments were an "exile" assignment to an undistinguished unit in Laon, in the Aisne district, and assignment to another undistinguished unit at Vannes, where he served under a rare Protestant general. Foch believed that these assignments were politically motivated tests of his loyalty to the republic; nevertheless, he staunchly refused to complain or accept help from sympathizers willing to intrigue on his part. Aisne, bordering as it did the Somme River and Belgium, ironically gave Foch critical knowledge of a soon-to-be-heavily-contested area.

These assignments gave a man of Foch's energies too little to do, so he turned his talents to writing. He published two books, *Principes de la Guerre* (*Principles of War*) in 1903 and *Conduite de la Guerre* (*Conduct of War*) in 1904. Built on his lectures at the École Supérieur de Guerre, these books were, in Foch's own words, more a statement of faith than of science. He professed the importance of moral spirit and the need for French armies to retain the offensive. In *Principes,* he wrote that "the goal of the military art is action. The rest is just literature."[3] Foch advocated will and morale to compensate for what he knew to be France's material shortcomings. These shortcomings were soon exacerbated by public policy. In 1905, the Third Republic, suspicious of the pernicious influence of the army on young men, reduced the term of mandatory military service from three years to two, effectively cutting by one-third the number of enlisted men available for military duty.

In 1907, Foch achieved the rank of brigadier general and was a finalist to return to the École Supérieur de Guerre as its commander. Foch, however, did not believe that having once been removed from the school for political reasons, he could now be named to run it. He had also heard rumors that his Catholicism had placed him out of favor with the men charged with making the decision. Nevertheless, on the advice of General Millet, Foch went to see Prime Minister Georges Clemenceau, famous as a stalwart defender of Alfred Dreyfus, to plead his case in person. Clemenceau told Foch that he would not command the École Supérieur de Guerre, but refused to tell him why. The meeting ended with Foch promising to send Clemenceau copies of his books so the prime minister could judge Foch for himself.

Clemenceau read the books carefully, then sent for Foch. At their second meeting, Clemenceau produced a secret file on Foch (written during his assignment in the Aisne district) that called him "a doubtful republican." The file also contained an earlier report that accused Foch of awarding higher grades to Catholics during his first assignment at the École Supérieur de Guerre. Just when it appeared that politics would again interfere, Clemenceau astonished Foch by telling him that he did not believe the report, nor did he care that Foch had a brother who was a rising star in the Society of Jesus. With war threatening, he wanted Foch to command the influential École Supérieur de Guerre. Foch, the devout Catholic, and Clemenceau, the equally strident anticlerical, shared an ardent love of France and an understanding of the need to prepare for the war to come. For Foch it was the start of a tumultuous relationship with Clemenceau and sweet revenge for his earlier humiliation. "After being thrown out [of the École Supérieur de Guerre] through the window," he boasted to a friend, "I came back through the front door."[4]

As commander of this distinguished school, Foch continued to stress the supreme importance of the offensive. French studies of Napoleon emphasized his penchant for the attack and his espousal of the principle that high morale could overcome significant disadvantages in matériel. Many French thinkers, including Foch, believed that French war planning in the years before 1870 had been too defensive, allowing Prussia to seize and maintain the initiative. Officers also stressed that French mobile field artillery gave soldiers the weaponry worthy of their innate courage, thereby making the offensive tactically possible. Now that France was part of the Triple Entente, which gave it important allies in Great Britain and Russia, France's strategic position had changed dramatically. Thus did French thinking become more offensive-minded in the decade before World War I.

Foch influenced a generation of officers, including France's true prophet of the cult of the offensive, Gen. Louis de Grandmaison, Director of Military Operations of the General Staff from 1908 to 1914. Foch was also in a position to evaluate the cream of the crop among French officers as they came through the École Supérieur de Guerre, both as students and as instructors. Once again, his lack of colonial service proved to be of great value, as his time in Paris gave him the chance to become acquainted with the important figures, political and military, with whom he eventually worked during the war.

These important figures included representatives of France's allies. In 1909, he met his British counterpart, Sir Henry Wilson, commander of the Army Staff College at Camberely. The two men developed a close friendship that paid important dividends both before and during the war. The francophile Wilson became a great admirer of Foch and invited him to Camberely where he introduced him to a colleague thus: "This fellow is going to command the Allied armies when the big war comes on."[5] Wilson went on to become Britain's Director of Military Operations and, eventually, Chief of the Imperial General Staff.

The close professional and personal relationship between Wilson and Foch was almost unparalleled in the annals of World War I. On the strategic level, the two men agreed on a likely German invasion of Belgium in the event of war and discussed possible ways of countering it. On Wilson's invitation, Foch visited England in 1910, 1911, and 1912, meeting most of Britain's senior military commanders. Wilson attended the wedding of Foch's eldest daughter, an unusual show of intimacy between professionals, especially men serving in different armies.

In 1910 Foch also paid an official visit to Russia on the occasion of the annual maneuvers of the Russian army. While there, he observed the Russian army firsthand and met frequently with Tsar Nicholas II. He left Russia unimpressed, convinced that Russian military methods were crude and that the Russian state was too brittle to survive a general war. As a result, Foch became an even more ardent supporter of close military links with Britain, especially the army. He discounted British arguments that the Royal Navy would be France's most important ally in the event of war, telling Wilson that the navy would not be worth one bayonet. Foch continued to push the British for firmer commitments to land a sizable expeditionary force on the continent upon the outbreak of hostilities.

Foch emerged as one of finalists for the job of chief of staff, alongside Generals Joffre, Castelnau, and Paul-Marie Pau. Among that group, Joffre had the least overt political and religious beliefs (Castelnau and Pau, like Foch, were open Catholics), and he was therefore the least controversial choice. Joffre soon asked for Foch to be named his first assistant. The new chief of staff was impressed with the intellect Foch had displayed at the École Supérieur de Guerre and believed that his "brain was of a higher order" than those of the other finalists. Foch had wanted the job of first assistant and the attendant chance to influence French grand strategy, but politics intruded once again. French War Minister and retired general Adolphe Messimy, a former Foch student, erased Foch's name from consideration for assistant chief of staff and held up Foch's promotion to three-star general. Joffre observed later that Messimy held "certain prejudices" against Foch, most likely his Catholicism and allegations of his antirepublicanism, which still had not dissipated.[6]

Foch, now sixty-one years old and passed over for both the chief of staff and assistant jobs, thought his career was all but over. Despite his connections to Joffre, Foch's next assignment was the marginally important job of directing the defenses of Nice. Soon after, however, the chief of staff's patronage did help him to acquire a much more important assignment, command of the Thirteenth Infantry Division in 1911. From there he moved on to command the Eighth Corps. In 1913, Joffre asked him to take over the critical Twentieth Corps, based at Nancy (where Manteuffel's bands had daily taunted the residents with "Retreat"), just south of Metz and very likely in the direct path of a future German assault. Foch carefully began to reorganize the corps, made up of two infantry divisions and one cavalry division, to prepare it for the leading role it was likely to have in a future war.

In February 1914, Foch saw for the first time a complete copy of Plan XVII, the French war plan. It called for a two-pronged offensive into Lorraine on either side of the heavily fortified Verdun-Toul line. The plan was bold, but it lacked clear strategic or operational objectives. Instead, it functioned more as a plan for concentration and deployment. It gave Joffre (who became commander-in-chief at the outbreak of war *ex officio*) maximum flexibility to seek a decisive battle with the Germans in Lorraine on the precise ground of his own choosing. Foch's Twentieth Corps was part of the Second Army under the command of General Castelnau. Foch's job under Plan XVII was to cover the southern extreme of the Second Army area of operations while the rest of the Second Army organized for the advance. Once organized, the Second Army was to lead the charge into Lorraine.

Foch instantly disliked Plan XVII. It violated three of his most important assumptions about the war to come. First, it assumed that French forces would be equal or superior in size to their German foes. Like most commanders of his day, Foch assumed the need to have significant numerical superiority in order for an attack to succeed. He doubted that the French could achieve sufficient supremacy of numbers in Lorraine. Second, Plan XVII assumed that Germany would respect Belgian neutrality. Foch had correctly surmised that they would not. Finally, it assumed that the main weight of German forces would come through the Ardennes, not the Low Countries.

Still, Foch's spirits were high. Should war break out, his Twentieth Corps was in an excellent position to reach Metz and allow him to liberate the city where he had listened to Manteuffel's German bands while studying to serve France. It was also the first real chance of his career to fight. For all of Foch's teaching and professing about the nature of war, his never having served in the colonies meant that he had never experienced the world of combat. Now he had a chance to put his theories into practice. He also had the full confidence of Joffre, who knew about Foch's emotional connection to Nancy and Metz. Joffre therefore believed that Foch, of all his generals, would fight the hardest in that area.

The assassination of Archduke Franz Ferdinand in Sarajevo on June 28 did not cause Foch any immediate concerns. He was on a two-week vacation at his estate in Brittany, and, like German Generals Helmuth von Moltke and Erich von Falkenhayn, saw no reason to cancel his personal plans. The delivery of the Austrian ultimatum to Serbia on July 23 changed the European situation drastically. Foch was soon recalled from leave to return to Twentieth Corps headquarters. The general European war, so long expected, was about to begin, and he was right in the center of it.

Despite his lack of colonial service and his trials at the hands of political authority, Foch found himself on the eve of war in command of the critically important Twentieth Corps, the spearhead of French forces. Foch's rise is a testimony to his patriotism, his energy, and his intelligence. As a result of his time at the École Supérieur de Guerre, he had a more extensive knowledge than most of the capabilities of many of his fellow generals, and he had forged important links to the British Army. These links soon proved critical to French survival as the crisis of 1914 broke and Ferdinand Foch finally faced the moment he had waited for his entire life.

Chapter 2

Foch and the Crisis of 1914

T HE ASSASSINATION of Archduke Franz Ferdi-
nand, downplayed at first by many European leaders, including
Foch, set off a train of events that few had foreseen and fewer
still could control. The alliance system that was supposed to
have safeguarded a balance of power in Europe instead dragged
all signatories into a conflagration that was not in their direct interests. For France to survive the opening months and avoid a
repetition of the disasters of the Franco-Prussian War, three conditions had to be met: Britain had to honor its Entente commitments or its promise to guarantee the neutrality of Belgium;
Italy had to remain neutral, despite its alliance to Germany and
Austria-Hungary, thus permitting France to focus exclusively on
Germany; and Russia, which Foch had discounted, had to mobilize quickly enough to draw German forces away from the
west. If any of these conditions failed to materialize, an out-
manned and outgunned France would be facing the greater
weight of a larger German army on disadvantageous terms.

Foch arrived at Metz on July 27 ready to liberate Lorraine per
Plan XVII, but instead received orders to move his units six

miles away from the border with Germany so that French forces would not accidentally precipitate a war. Foch, with his love of the offensive, disregarded the order and prepared to move into the heights around Nancy, though he obeyed the spirit of the order by directing that under no circumstances were his troops to enter Germany. The next day, Germany issued an unreasonable demand that France cede the fortresses around Verdun and Toul. The ultimatum, which Germany knew France would refuse, was designed to give German diplomats the slightest veneer of a justification for a declaration of war. France immediately rejected the demand and prepared to mobilize for war in the event either of a German invasion or a declaration of war between Germany and Russia, France's Entente partner. Thus the assassination of an Austrian archduke led to war between Germany, Belgium, Britain, and France.

Foch and Henry Wilson had already guessed the general outlines of German strategy. As they had predicted five years earlier, Germany invaded Belgium, crossing the border on August 4. Still, Foch's energies were absorbed in the Lorraine region and he was slow to realize that he was falling into a trap. The German Schlieffen Plan intended to engage and hold the French First and Second Armies in Lorraine using units from the German Sixth and Seventh Armies, while the main thrust of German forces (the German First through Fifth Armies) swung through Belgium and west of Paris. The plan was intended to work like a swinging gate, with the center "post" planted just north of Foch's Twentieth Corps. Therefore, the more progress the French Second Army made to the east, the farther they would be from Paris, the ultimate target of German planning.

Although he had long anticipated a violation of Belgian neutrality, it took Foch nearly a month to realize the true nature of German intentions. French obsession with the "Lost Provinces" of Alsace and Lorraine had led to a fixation, reflected in Plan XVII, on France's eastern areas. The German demand that France surrender Verdun and Toul only reinforced an eastern outlook. Foch himself personified these obsessions; while his head had predicted Germany's march through Belgium, his heart remained focused on Lorraine. Thus, as French forces moved east, German forces moved quickly to their north and toward the French rear, threatening Second Army's communications.

Moreover, it took Second Army commander Castelnau, Foch's superior, and First Army commander Auguste Dubail longer to prepare than they had envisioned. French politicians further impeded their progress because they wanted to be sure that Germany would be seen as the aggressor—hence the lack of immediate offensive action and the order to move back six miles from the frontier. Foch's Twentieth Corps was the first element of Second Army to be readied, and Foch soon grew impatient with the delay. He wanted to attack quickly both to assume the cherished offensive and because he believed that by attacking he could disrupt the timing of German operations. Frustrated, he wrote to his wife, "After fifteen days of inactivity, I feel like a caged lion."[1]

By mid-August, however, Foch, like most other French commanders, was still trying to discern German intentions. Germany had indeed violated Belgian neutrality, but it remained unclear whether the Belgian thrust was the main action or an elaborate feint. Britain responded as France had hoped, with a declaration of war against Germany for violating Belgian neutrality and for threatening ports on the English Channel. Britain quickly dispatched its small professional army, the British Expeditionary Force (BEF), to the continent under the command of Sir John French, though French came to Europe determined that he would exercise his command independent of the wishes of his French allies. Italy, moreover, gave every indication that it would indeed sit on the sidelines. For its part, Russia mobilized faster than almost anyone, including Foch, believed possible.

After two weeks of inactivity, Foch received permission on August 14 to begin his advance. Castelnau had originally intended for the Sixteenth and Fifteenth Corps, on Foch's right, to lead the assault. Those corps, however, did not make much progress. Foch, on the other hand, had gained ten miles in five days, despite heavy French casualties and significant German advantages in men and in heavy guns. His forces entered Lorraine as liberators, with bands playing and celebrations in every hamlet they entered.

Foch's ability to move forward while other corps commanders had not confirmed his belief that the superior will of the French soldier, combined with the fierce determination of an aggressive commander, could counteract German material superiority. Unfortunately, his position was not as strong as he believed it to be. He did not know that the Germans had eight corps in the area, not the six that had been reported to him by French intelligence. Foch also did not know of the valuable aerial reconnaissance that German observation aircraft had provided to German army commanders. His enemy therefore had far more information on his positions than he had on the German positions. Moreover, the Schlieffen Plan never intended for the operations in Lorraine to be much more than a sideshow, meaning that much of the costly French advance was of marginal strategic value.

From an operational standpoint, Foch's advance had been too successful, placing his corps too far ahead to offer support to the Fifteenth and Sixteenth Corps. Seeing an opportunity, the German Sixth Army savagely counterattacked the two exposed corps on August 20. The Fifteenth and Sixteenth Corps soon retreated, leaving Foch's Twentieth Corps dangerously exposed and leaving a gap between First and Second Armies. Still, he continued with plans to attack the Morhange Heights, even though the two corps closest to him were in full retreat. Castelnau, seeing the precarious position of his Second Army, ordered Foch to give up his plans for Morhange and fall back so that the three corps of Second Army could support one another. Foch claimed not to have received the order and was preparing to move forward when the Germans hit him first, causing heavy casualties. Joffre repeated Castelnau's order to retreat and Foch finally obeyed.

The bloody disaster at Morhange caused considerable strain in both military and political circles. The Parisian daily newspaper *Le Matin* reported on the defeat at Morhange thus:

Companies, battalions, passed in indescribable disorder. Mixed in with the soldiers were women carrying children in their arms or pushing little carts in front of them, girls in their Sunday best, old people, carrying or dragging a bizarre mixture of objects. Entire regiments were falling back in disorder. One had the impression that discipline had completely collapsed. Nonetheless all these units had regular cadres and belonged to the active army.[2]

Such a bloody defeat of the professional army would have to be explained. Castelnau blamed Foch for willingly disobeying a direct order to retreat. Tensions rose between the two men, and, despite their similar Catholic, Pyrenean backgrounds, they soon became bitter enemies.

Joffre's report to French President Raymond Poincaré on the battles near Morhange criticized Foch for moving too far too fast, thus causing unnecessary French casualties. In light of later developments in the war, a commander criticizing a subordinate for moving too fast seems odd. Still, Joffre remained impressed with Foch. He did not repeat to the president Castelnau's charge that Foch had willingly disobeyed an order. Reckless offensives, heavy losses, and possible insubordination all notwithstanding, Foch had still advanced while others had held or retreated. Joffre praised Foch's "splendid courage and unshakeable confidence," and in a telegram to the minister of war he lauded Foch's "incontestable superiority from the point of view of character and military ability."[3]

These words were not idle praise. Joffre was then in the process of removing dozens of senior French commanders, including many close friends like Charles Lanrezac. By the time the purges were over, Joffre had removed nearly one in three members of the French high command, including three army commanders, seven corps commanders, thirty-four divisional commanders, and fourteen brigade commanders. He assigned so many officers to the rear echelon town of Limoges that a new verb, *Limoger* (meaning to be removed from one's job for incompetence) entered the French military lexicon. Foch, with his contagious confidence and courage, not only remained in

Joffre's good graces, he soon became Joffre's most trusted lieutenant.

Having completed his retreat in front of Morhange by the end of August, Foch soon came to realize the extreme gravity of the French situation. With his local actions over, he began to see the larger picture. German forces had completed the capture of the Belgian fortresses of Liège and Namur and had entered France. They had pushed four French armies, the BEF, and the 110,000-man Belgian army away from the Franco-Belgian border and were threatening Paris. Foch now understood that his actions in the east had been a diversion at best, a trap at worst. The real threat was to the capital. Foch also learned that his son, Germain, and his son-in-law, the promising young Capt. Charles Bécourt, had fallen in combat on the Franco-Belgian frontier. He took the news stoically, saying to his staff, "I can do nothing more for him. Perhaps I can still do something for France. Back to work."[4]

Despite the controversies over Morhange, on August 29, Joffre asked Foch to leave Twentieth Corps to take command of a group of unattached units between Fernand de Langle de Cary's Fourth Army on his right and Louis Franchet d'Esperey's Fifth Army on his left. This group, soon reorganized as the Ninth Army, sat in a critical position just south of the Marne River and east of Paris. Foch had to restructure completely this jumbled grouping of units, many of which had been in full retreat for weeks. He replaced officers, reestablished lines of communication, and ordered that "infantry was to be economized, artillery freely used, and every foot of ground gained was to be at once organized for defense."[5] This comment reveals that Foch had learned an important lesson from the disaster at Morhange: French élan, however magnificent, could not win a war without the right support.

Foch took with him to the Ninth Army a young staff officer, Maxime Weygand, who became his confidant and alter ego. "Weygand, c'est moi," Foch often declared, and he frequently referred to his young assistant as "my encyclopedia." The Belgian-born Weygand was himself an interesting character. His exact background remains a mystery to this day. Despite his foreign birth, he secured an appointment to the French military academy at St. Cyr, fueling the speculation that he must have had prominent anonymous patrons. Before and during the war, rumors frequently circulated that he was the illegitimate son of Belgian King Leopold II or the Emperor Maximilian of Mexico (thus his first name).

Joffre had been the first to recognize Weygand's talents and before the war he had sent him to the Twentieth Corps as a staff officer. When Foch took command of the Ninth Army, he had to choose between Weygand and another officer for the job of his chief of staff. Foch later recalled how he came to choose Weygand: "I will take the senior. If he is no good to me, back he goes to his regiment in a few days' time." It proved to be a fortuitous happenstance that Weygand was senior to the other officer. "I was to keep him nine years," Foch noted.[6]

Weygand remained with Foch throughout the war, always near him and frequently to be seen whispering with his chief. The two were an ideal match. Weygand was an efficient staff officer, turning Foch's general exhortations into specific orders and battle plans. Foch provided the vision and the charisma, while Weygand performed the work needed to turn Foch's grand ideas into reality. When visitors to Foch's headquarters complemented him, Foch frequently pointed to Weygand and replied, "Me? I do nothing—he does all the work."[7] Weygand ended the war as a brigadier general and, like Foch, lived in Brittany with his Breton wife. In May 1940, he was recalled to command the French Army in the futile hopes that he could work some of Foch's magic in a renewed time of crisis.

Joffre had immediate plans for the Foch-Weygand team. The French commander-in-chief quickly divined that the French Ninth and Fourth armies had an opportunity to halt German momentum by striking the First and Second Armies near the Marne. Through aerial reconnaissance reports, Joffre determined that the two German armies (commanded by Alexander von Kluck and Karl von Bülow, respectively) were heading to the east of Paris, not to the west, as originally believed. Overextension and a rapid Russian advance into East Prussia had caused German commander Helmuth von Moltke to abandon his plans to invest Paris from the west.

Joffre determined that a rapid strike into the flanks of the exhausted German troops might stop them in their tracks. The moment had come for France to turn the tide or lose the war. Joffre's proclamation of September 5 read: "At the moment when the battle upon which hangs the fate of France is about to begin, all must remember that the time for looking back is past; every effort must be concentrated on attacking and throwing the enemy back. . . . Under present conditions, no weakness can be tolerated."[8]

The French situation was indeed grave. The stunning German advance to within twenty-five miles of the capital led to the evacuation of the French government from Paris to Bordeaux. Gen. Joseph Galliéni, recently named commander of the Paris military district, began to prepare the city for a long siege. Furthermore, relations between Joffre and BEF commander Sir John French were at their nadir after Joffre complained to the British government that the BEF had fought with too little enthusiasm and retreated with too much ardor. That complaint brought a visit to Field Marshal French from British Secretary of State for War Lord Kitchener, who ordered French to fill in the vital gap between Paris and the French Fifth Army. The BEF commander was furious at Joffre, and the two commanders-in-chief barely spoke to one another during this crucial time.

Foch was entirely in accord with Joffre's plan and relished the chance to resume the offensive. Still, his first attacks did not proceed well. He found his Ninth Army confined on his left by the impassable marshes of St. Gond; on his right, he had a twelve-mile gap that was covered by only one division of cavalry. By the morning of September 8, Foch found himself in danger of being routed. A German attack surprised four of his divisions, all of which quickly began to retreat, leaving Foch almost alone in his advance headquarters at Pleurs. Typical of Foch, he was able to halt the retreat after about five miles and regroup his forces for a renewed attack. Then he wrote the message that began the Foch legend: "My center is giving way, my right is in retreat. Situation excellent. I attack." Later the same day, he told one of his corps commanders, "You say you cannot hold on, and that you cannot withdraw, so the only thing left is to attack."[9]

The Battle of the Marne proved to be one of the decisive battles of the twentieth century. More than 1,200,000 men were engaged on each side. The Germans, exhausted from constant marching and fighting, decided to abandon the Schlieffen Plan. The Russian advance into East Prussia had caused Moltke to pull troops away from France and send them east. Foch's attacks had opened a gap between the two German armies. Bülow ordered a retreat to shorten the lines and maintain contact between the two armies.

The French attacks on the Marne accomplished what Joffre had desired. They forced the German First and Second Armies to withdraw back to the Aisne River. There would be no siege of Paris as in 1870. France had regained an area roughly 100 miles long and fifty miles deep. Joffre and Galliéni received most of the credit for the "Miracle of the Marne" and shared the title of "savior of France." Galliéni captured the attention of a public desperate for heroes by commandeering hundreds of Parisian taxicabs to move two brigades (roughly 6,000 men) to the front. Foch himself credited Joffre for his fast responses to the opportunity provided by aerial reconnaissance. Foch did, however, receive a share of the credit when War Minister Alexander Millerand awarded him the Legion of Honor, the same award Napoleon had once bestowed on Foch's grandfather.

On September 13, Foch entered Châlons and found that the Germans had destroyed most of the city during their retreat. He understood that the French armies were exhausted from the Battle of the Marne, but he was frustrated when Joffre forbade him from pursuing the retreating Germans. He was angry at the German destruction of Châlons and no doubt vengeful after the tragic loss of a son and son-in-law on the same day. His offensive spirit, however, remained as dogged as ever. He later told Gen. Louis de Maud'huy, whom he had first met at school in Metz, "I only know three ways of fighting: attack, hold on, and run away. I forbid the last. Choose between the first two."[10]

The Marne had been a bloody, confusing, sprawling battle larger than anyone had thought possible. The management of these ever-larger battlefields was a task for which the commanders of 1914 were not well prepared. This new kind of war required a new kind of general. As historian Hew Strachan has recently argued, "The quality most urgently required of a general in such circumstances, devoid of information for long periods and too often unable to resolve his tension with activity, was an inner certainty, a belief in ultimate success, a bloody-minded obstinacy."

As Strachan notes, these were qualities that Foch had "in abundance."[11] They came from his absolute faith in the righteousness of the French cause and his belief that France could not be beaten as long as it believed in the eventuality of its triumph.

After the Battle of the Marne, Foch found his Ninth Army on the south bank of the Aisne River. Oddly enough, he was now opposite Laon, the place of his "exile" assignment in 1901. Paris had been saved, but the situation was still dire. Germany was in control of much of the northeastern portion of France, which was also the nation's industrial core. One in ten Frenchmen was living under German occupation. Further to the east, however, the situation was somewhat brighter. The great fortresses of Verdun, Toul, and Épinal were still under French control, mostly because they were not primary targets of German operations.

As the smoke cleared from the Battle of the Marne, Joffre and Foch assessed their recent experiences. Foch concluded that frontal assaults on reinforced positions nearly always failed. French morale alone did not overcome German steel. He and Joffre concluded that their tired troops could not be expected to attempt more frontal assaults in the near future, especially since the Germans had begun to dig in on the high ground near the Aisne River. On September 27, Foch learned that France had exhausted its supply of shells for the mainstay of its field artillery, the 75mm gun. Accordingly, he ordered all units to prepare to defend. Trench warfare had begun.

As a result of his conduct at the Marne, Foch's reputation soared. On September 24, Joffre asked that Foch be named his successor in case of accident. The request, if approved, would have superseded an official letter of appointment to Galliéni that named him Joffre's successor. This incident is illustrative of the continuing intrusion of domestic politics into Foch's career and the conduct of army operations. Joffre's relations with Parliament had grown quite tense, largely as a result of Joffre's declaration of near-supreme powers in the "Zone of the Armies" that covered most of eastern France. Joffre had banned parliamentarians from entering the zone and even threatened to arrest several of France's most important politicians (including President Raymond Poincaré and Senate Army Committee Chairman Georges Clemenceau) if they dared to enter without his permission. French politicians therefore saw Joffre's request for Foch to be his successor as an attempt to solidify his position by naming the loyal Foch over his more popular rival and Marne hero, Galliéni. For his part, Galliéni had been privately critical of Joffre's failure to exploit his Marne success.

Being associated so closely with Joffre thus caused Foch significant problems, especially since Foch had already had several run-ins with French politicians. Parliament and President Poincaré were unwilling to remove the letter of appointment from the popular, republican Galliéni. The request to replace Galliéni with Foch was thus denied, but Foch received the title of assistant chief of staff, the same job he had been denied three years earlier.

Allegations and suspicions regarding Foch's political leanings remained and grew to outlandish proportions. Fourth Army commander Gen. Maurice Sarrail, France's most overtly political general and the darling of left-leaning French politicians, even accused Joffre and Foch of planning a coup d'état. Sarrail believed that the Joffre-Foch team would mean "the return of im-

perialism and the end of the republic." When Sarrail tried to en-
list the support of one of Foch's deputies in a plot to remove him,
the deputy instead told Foch of Sarrail's intrigues. Foch duly informed Joffre, who put the matter to rest, though the incident
did nothing to improve Joffre's relations with Parliament or with
Sarrail, whom he tried to remove from command shortly thereafter.[12]

In light of the ridiculous Sarrail incident, Foch's attitude toward politics and politicians deserves some mention. He came to
distrust and dislike politicians not because he disliked the republic, but for the standard soldier's complaint that they inter-
fered too much in matters they did not understand. As Foch
later wrote: "The very situation of an officer should prohibit
him, whether in time of peace or war, from mixing up in the
struggles and quarrels of politics. His professional value can reveal itself only in the field of action, before men of the same
trade, his peers or superiors; it cannot be estimated by political
men."[13]

For similar reasons, he held an equal contempt for most jour-
nalists, whom he saw as men of words, not action. Far from plot-
ting a coup, Foch so disliked politics that he stayed as far away
from political affairs as possible. After the war, he declined numerous entreaties to run for public office. He was, however, as-
tute enough not to challenge politicians as openly as Joffre
frequently did. Unlike Joffre, Foch received politicians at his
headquarters, if reluctantly.

Foch thus survived yet another political challenge. The challenge of how to dislodge German positions on French soil, however, persisted. With frontal assaults temporarily out of the
question because of exhausted troops and shortages of artillery
shells, an alternative had to be found. Foch and Joffre decided
instead to try to turn the German lines by moving around their
right. The Germans had come to the same conclusion and began
to attempt flanking movements of their own. Thus began the in-
appropriately named "Race to the Sea," which was really a series
of turning maneuvers that continued until the armies ran out of

favorable real estate both at the English Channel and at the Swiss border.

Foch's new assignment as assistant chief of staff carried with it command of an army group comprising two eastern armies, including Castelnau's Second Army. Thus Castelnau, his former commander and the man who had accused him of disobeying orders, was now his subordinate. The snub to Castelnau of placing him under the man he had blamed for the disaster at Morhange was intentional. Joffre had given Foch the challenge of changing Castelnau's habit of retreating, and thereby reinvigorating the morale of the Second Army. Foch did so in his first meeting as Army Group Commander. He rejected Castelnau's request to retire behind the Somme River. When Castelnau complained, Foch surprised him by producing a written order to hold his position and telling him curtly, "I take entire responsibility; my decision is irrevocable. Here is the order in writing."[14]

The other part of Foch's new assignment was the command to organize British, French, and Belgian forces as they "raced" toward the sea. "Go and see the situation," Joffre told him, "and do your best."[15] Again, Foch was the right man for the job. Whereas Joffre's relations with the BEF and the Belgians had been tense at best, Foch was on friendly terms with several of the BEF's commanders, including its commander-in-chief, Sir John French. Thanks to his years as commander of the École Supérieur de Guerre, he had long-standing personal relationships with several allied commanders. Upon these relationships, Foch built a trust that saw the Allied armies through yet another crisis.

Chapter 3

The Lessons of Modern Warfare: The Flanders Campaigns

F ERDINAND FOCH arrived in the Flanders region of Belgium to find a chaotic and confused situation in the north. He had also left the Ninth Army with a heavy heart. Before departing, Foch had to inform his wife and family of the deaths of Germain Foch and Charles Bécourt on August 22 in Belgium. Foch was not alone in his grief. His friend of nearly forty years, General Millet, the man who had suggested the audience with Georges Clemenceau that had led to Foch's command of the École Supérieur de Guerre, had also lost a son in the early weeks of the war. Foch's letter of condolence to Millet reveals much of Foch's mental state as he took on his new assignment: "For myself I try to find support in remembering my duty, but not without difficulty. The cruel sacrifices which we are enduring ought not to remain sterile. I shall work with all the energy of which I am capable, absolutely confident of the issue of the fight, with the mercy of God helping us."[1]

He spoke little of his loss, aware as he was that everyone in France was suffering. Still, he carried that loss with him and converted it into a determination to see the war out to a successful conclusion and thereby give meaning to his family's suffering. The letter also demonstrates Foch's abiding faith that he was fighting with providential blessing, a belief that sustained him through several periods of crisis.

But before he could determine how best to apply his energies to the series of flanking movements in the north, Foch first needed to gain a better understanding of the situation he was facing in Flanders. The sixty-two-year-old general immediately set to work, covering 550 miles in just fifty-seven hours and meeting with as many divisional commanders as possible. He soon appreciated that the Allied armies faced a dual challenge: they would have to prevent outflanking maneuvers by the Germans on the Allied left, while at the same time devoting sufficient resources to stop Germany from seizing the Channel ports.

The indefatigable Foch responded with characteristic action. Within three days of taking his new assignment, he directed that French forces prepare the defense of the Channel ports, as German seizure of those cities would greatly endanger communications with Great Britain. He also rushed French marines under the command of Pierre Ronarc'h to the Belgian city of Dixmude on the Yser River and gave them explicit orders to hold the city at all costs. These marines provided needed succor to the exhausted and retreating Belgians.

The need to support the Belgians demonstrates another challenge Foch faced: the intricate problems of alliance warfare. Despite the diplomatic alliance between Great Britain and France, there had been remarkably little joint military planning in the years prior to the war. The Entente Cordiale had produced only the most general of military understandings. Nor had the war itself drawn Britain and France any closer together. BEF commander Sir John French was jealously protective of his strategic and operational independence and was still fuming at Joffre for questioning his courage in August. French also grew anxious at the prospect of losing the Channel ports and gave occasional indications of retreating along his line of communications to those ports. Foch needed to keep the BEF's attention focused on the battle in Flanders and dissuade John French from any thoughts of abandoning the fight.

French had grown anxious because the BEF had been badly bloodied in the early stages of the war. Alone among the Great Powers, Britain did not have mandatory military service in the prewar years, preferring to rely on the dominance of the Royal Navy and the high quality of Britain's professional volunteer soldiers. By the early fall of 1914, that core of experienced professionals had suffered unprecedented casualties and there were as yet no definitive plans to replace them with a continental-style conscript army. Even as plans evolved, military leaders knew it would take months, maybe years, to train and equip sufficient numbers of eager, if inexperienced, British volunteers. Thus French saw Britain's small army dwindling before his eyes and he did not care to preside over its final demise. Loss of the army would, of course, endanger the entire empire, most notably Ireland, where tensions had been building in the years before the war. French therefore grew stubborn, occasionally lethargic, and often uncooperative with his continental Allies.

As the Dixmude episode shows, Foch also had to work with the Belgians, another nominal French ally with whom there had been little to no prewar military cooperation. The Belgians had traditionally relied on their adherence to neutrality and their once-impressive system of fortifications for security. The former proved to be of little value in the face of an advancing German army, and the latter was no match for modern, custom-designed German artillery. The Belgian king, Albert I, was commander-in-chief of the Belgian army, which he had purposefully built as a defensive force. Like the BEF, the Belgian army was tired, suffering from terrible early losses, and thoroughly unprepared for the kind of war it found itself fighting.

Out of this situation, Joffre wanted Foch to create unity of command. Foch faced the additional problem of being junior in rank to the two men he was supposed to command. John French, a field marshal, bristled at taking orders from a general, and a French general at that. Still, as long as the French, British, and Belgian armies remained three separate forces, Germany would hold a critical strategic advantage. Somehow, three armies with divergent interests had to be welded into a semblance of a coherent whole.

Nor were the Allies in complete agreement over what to do next. The Belgians desperately wanted to hold on to a small strip of their homeland based around the city of Ypres. The BEF wanted to retain contact with the Channel ports. France wanted to secure Paris and drive the invading Germans out of their nation. While these goals were not necessarily mutually exclusive, neither were they exactly complementary.

Merging all these interests would be a tremendous challenge. Joffre, with his stubbornness and impatience for diplomacy, could not have done it. Foch, on the other hand, was just the man for the job. He had previous professional and personal contacts with almost all of the senior British and Belgian officers. Most important, he had a long-standing and amicable relationship with French. He also knew that whatever Joffre may have envisioned, he could not give orders to commanders of different nationalities. "Each army," he later wrote in recalling his thinking in 1914, "has its own spirit and tradition; each has to satisfy the requirements of its own government; and the latter, in turn, has its own particular needs and interests to consider."[2] He would have to act instead through inspiration, persuasion, and personal example.

The first and most urgent target for Foch's art of persuasion was BEF commander French. Foch met with French and his old friend Sir Henry Wilson just four days after beginning his new assignment. He found French despondent and pessimistic. Foch took the hand of his old comrade-in-arms and told him, "The British Army has never drawn back in its history. You have the honor of England in your hands as I have that of France. The entire world has its eyes on us. Even should this act result in my own death, I have come to give you my word as a soldier that I will not take one step back. I want you to give me your word and it is your duty to give it to me."[3]

French was deeply moved by Foch's entreaty and agreed not to withdraw to the north. Foch then implored him to ask the Royal Navy to move a squadron off the coast of Ostend in the hopes of slowing down any German advance along the Belgian coast.

He then met with King Albert and found Albert desperate to hold on to the small strip of Belgium remaining to him, whatever the costs. Albert, whose spirit and energy rivaled that of any Allied commander, proved to be every bit as tenacious as Foch himself. Foch agreed to support him and asked him to prepare the sluice gates in front of the Belgian line to be opened, thereby flooding the Flanders plains with a two-mile-wide swath of salt water. He ordered French forces to retire to a line east of the Nieuport-Dixmude Railroad and ordered the French sluice gates prepared as well. The move was a drastic (and temporary) solution, but combined with the Royal Navy movements, the water inundations promised to give the Allies enough time to reorganize in an emergency. The flat ground of Flanders, Foch knew, had few natural obstacles; therefore, it would be necessary to create them. Digging in also proved to be much more difficult in Flanders than in the chalky soil of eastern France, because water tables were often as high as just a few inches under the ground in places. Trenches would therefore be no deeper than a few feet, filled with water, and would provide only minimal shelter from rifle fire and artillery.

Winston Churchill later wrote that Foch "alone possessed the size and combative energy to prevent the severance of the French and British armies."[4] By size, Churchill meant a charisma and stature much greater than Foch's five-foot, seven-inch frame might have indicated. More than size, Foch possessed an ability to understand the BEF's basic needs and how best to respond to them. He also had the energy and diplomatic skills necessary to persuade the British to see the war his way. On October 17, Foch met with David Lloyd George, then serving as Chancellor of the Exchequer. The future British War Minister and Prime Minister left impressed with Foch's strategic vision. As noted above,

Churchill, then serving as First Lord of the Admiralty, also developed confidence in Foch.

Despite their confidence in him, Foch's tactical and operational views of the war at this stage did not entirely conform to reality. Although he was almost uniquely gifted among French officers in his ability to form and manage alliances, he was not able to divorce his operational thinking from a lifetime spent teaching about the virtues of the offensive. Unrealistic as it seems today, Foch was planning to reorganize Allied forces for a joint offensive that would drive through Lille and from there onto Brussels. The plan reflected Foch's abiding belief in the power of the offensive. His experiences thus far in the war might have convinced him that such grandiose offensives were not feasible, but they did not. In actuality, Allied forces were far too weak to consider such an advance, especially as German reinforcements began to come to Flanders after the fortresses near the Belgian city of Antwerp surrendered on October 9. Still, his view was infinitely more sensible than that of John French, who thought the Flanders terrain was ideal ground for cavalry actions.

Instead of attacking, Foch soon found himself defending. A fierce German offensive began, consisting of two overlapping phases: the Battle of Yser from October 17 to November 1 and the First Battle of Ypres from October 21 to November 12. The German commander, Erich von Falkenhayn, unconstrained by the needs of alliance warfare, had planned two major offensives, with the heaviest use of artillery to date. He hoped to turn the French left flank and then proceed along the Channel. For this effort, Falkenhayn had nineteen fresh divisions for the attacks. Allied forces, especially the Belgians, were still disorganized and unprepared.

King Albert responded to the crisis with urgent action. He posted marksmen to the rear and gave them orders to shoot retreating Belgian soldiers; he threatened to court-martial officers who reported sick; and he reassigned his staff officers to the line. Understanding the gravity of the situation, Foch abandoned his offensive plans around the Yser River and redirected elements of the French Forty-Second Infantry Division to come to the aid of the Belgians. On October 24 alone, Falkenhayn launched fifteen separate assaults, establishing positions across the Yser. On October 27, the Belgians completed the water inundations and thus secured their left flank. They had held, but just barely.

Farther to the south, Foch responded to the German attacks in characteristic fashion: he launched repeated counterattacks of his own. The French Eighth Army, under Gen. Victor d'Urbal, attacked to the northeast of Ypres. While the French took heavy casualties without gaining much ground, Foch thought the offensives had been a success, as they took pressure off the beleaguered Belgians, disrupted German timing, and shamed the BEF, whose command structure was then planning a retreat, into taking the offensive themselves.

Foch's counterattacks notwithstanding, the Ypres Offensive once again scared Sir John French, who feared that his BEF could be swallowed up by the German advance. French told Foch, "There is nothing left to do but die." Foch calmly replied, "We must stand firm first. We can die afterwards."[5] Foch went to Ypres, climbing the tower of the city's medieval cloth tower in order to get a better look at the battlefield. Even in the face of the German attacks, Foch completed a complicated reorganization of forces to allow the British, Belgians, and French to each have their own contiguous areas. He also established nightly meetings with Wilson, who served as a high-level liaison between Foch and French.

Foch had no new answers to the tactical problems of the 1914 battlefield, but neither did anyone else. The *Times* of London's military correspondent insightfully described Foch's strategy as the "triumph of obstinacy."[6] Foch worked best at the strategic level, bringing British, Belgian, and French efforts into coordination and, perhaps most important, bolstering the confidence of the faltering John French. In early November, seventy-five of the BEF's eighty-four infantry battalions were at less than one-third of their August strength. The Kaiser himself had arrived at the German lines outside Ypres, having already been told that the city had fallen. The desperate situation facing the Allies notwithstanding, Foch forbade French from retreating. "The Kaiser wishes to enter Ypres," he told French. "He shall not enter. I don't wish it."[7] Foch earned French's loyalty when he turned down an offer from Lord Kitchener to replace French with Sir Ian Hamilton.

Mutual exhaustion and the onset of winter, more than anything Foch did, stopped the German advances. The battle had cost the old British army some of its most important veteran leadership. Recent estimates suggest that the BEF lost 50,000 men. France lost in excess of 60,000 men, and German losses may have been as high as 130,000 men. The Allies could claim victory, but only in the sense that they had prevented the Germans from entering Ypres.

Still, for Foch the saving of Ypres was a great personal victory. He had accomplished the improbable: he had fused together a true coalition that worked together to deny the Germans control of the continental side of the English Channel. King Albert developed tremendous confidence in him, proclaiming, "That man could make the dead fight."[8] For his service in saving the BEF, King George V came to France personally to award Foch the Grand Cross of the Order of Bath. Although the honor was indeed flattering, Foch appreciated the larger significance: the award carried with it an important vote of confidence from Great Britain's most senior leaders. Many British leaders had grown disenchanted with French. Supporting Foch allowed them to subordinate French without having to take the drastic step of changing commanders-in-chief.

Thus, in January 1915, the Allies agreed to give Foch the title of Commander of the Armies of the North, conferring on him a nominal joint authority not held by any other Allied commander, including Joffre. Foch found himself in an area with little precedent and he had to develop haphazard solutions to the new challenges of modern alliance warfare. His new title fell far short of bestowing upon him the powers of a commander-in-chief and did not compensate for his relatively junior rank. He was certainly in no position to give orders to a Belgian king. Nor did the "victory" at Ypres bolster Sir John French's confidence. Foch's support in the face of Kitchener's offer to replace him cemented their personal relationship, but French continued to have mood swings that called into question his fitness for such an important command. During the course of 1915, confidence in him continued to wane, leading to his replacement by Sir Douglas Haig in December.

Tactically and operationally, the problems in front of Foch were just as daunting. With German armies on French and Belgian soil, defensive stalemates like Ypres would not win the war. On the most fundamental level, Foch and his fellow Allied commanders were caught in an unsolvable dilemma: to end the German occupation, the Allies had to resume the offensive, yet Ypres had conclusively shown how dangerous and costly assaults against prepared positions had become. Foch continued to believe that only renewed offensives could dislodge the Germans and drive them back, although he also realized that "war against fortified positions will increasingly become our lot."[9] He further understood that the German trenches were "veritable citadels" and that France lacked the large stocks of heavy artillery needed to overcome them.[10]

Foch was therefore caught in a quandary he could not resolve. His experiences in the early weeks of the war seemed to undermine a lifetime of teaching. The offensive had not proven to be the master of the battlefield. In fact, just the reverse had come true—the defense was now supreme. Still, Foch, like Joffre, remained optimistic that a well-planned offensive, adequately supported by heavy artillery, could achieve a breakthrough and a rapid end to the war. He continued to believe that the war would be won or lost in France, and he objected to any proposals for operations in the Middle East or the Balkans. To that end, Foch spent the early months of 1915 planning an offensive against Vimy Ridge in the Artois region.

Once again, however, the Germans beat him to the punch. Falkenhayn attacked Ypres again on April 22, 1915. At this battle, the Second Battle of Ypres, the Germans used a new weapon, chlorine gas, to open a four-mile gap in the Allied lines. German prisoners had warned the Allies of the new weapon, and one of them had even been captured with a crude respirator. Still, Foch had made no preparations for dealing with gas. Curiously, neither had Falkenhayn. He was unable to take advantage of the gap because he had devoted no reserves for exploitation. Though Foch later credited the speedy arrival of three French divisions for saving Ypres, the truth is that the Germans were uncharacteristically unprepared to build upon the early successes of the offensive.

Still, the events of April 22 caught Foch quite by surprise. The fog and friction of the modern battlefield made the personal, Napoleonic style of command Foch had preached virtually impossible. "One knew nothing, one could know nothing, and if one waited until the next day it meant a break-through."[11] The attacks struck most forcefully at the British, who were at the same time landing troops on the beaches of Turkey's Gallipoli Peninsula. French, buoyed by Foch, ordered bloody counterattacks that predictably failed to regain the lost ground. French soon recommended withdrawal to the west of the Ypres Canal, an action that would have given the town of Ypres to the Germans. Foch overrode him, and on April 30 and May 1, he ordered more costly counteroffensives.

Foch wanted to conduct counteroffensives around Ypres while simultaneously proceeding with his planned offensive against the Vimy Ridge salient north of Arras. Foch's aggressive spirit was too much, even for Joffre. The French commander overrode Foch and ordered the offensives around Ypres halted. Joffre directed that Foch send forces earmarked for those attacks to Arras. The Allied salient around Ypres had been dented, but it had once again held, albeit at great cost.

Foch now pinned his hopes for penetrating the German lines near Arras. Just north of that town sat a salient that bulged into the area where the First British Army and Tenth French Army lines converged. Inside the German lines sat the Vimy Ridge, three hills of 160, 140, and 132 meters height, ranging north to south. Foch envisioned an intense artillery preparation that he hoped would cut paths through the German wire, followed by a direct assault on the German positions. Once dislodged from their trenches, Foch believed, French forces could achieve the long-awaited breakthrough and then outflank the Germans from the north and the south simultaneously. Once the French achieved this, Foch argued, he could win the war in three months!

On May 3, Foch's artillery began a six-day bombardment. On May 9, the artillery stopped. After a two-minute silence, French troops left their trenches and began to cross the thousand yards of No Man's Land. They soon discovered that the French artillery had failed to cut the German wire. Shortages of high explosive shells had forced the French to rely instead on antipersonnel shrapnel shells, which lacked the power to do significant damage to barbed wire. Still, French troops pressed on through two tangled lines of wire, capturing Hill 160 and the near slope of Hill 140.

French troops quickly found that their progress was possible in part because the Germans has simply retired to another line of trenches farther back. French progress came to a halt. By May 15, the opportunity for even a limited breakthrough had passed. Still, Foch ordered the Tenth Army to continue the attacks and to prepare the cavalry to be ready to pass through the anticipated break in the German lines. By mid-June, France had suffered 102,000 casualties (twice the German losses) and had advanced no more than three miles. German reinforcements were already in place and were arriving much faster than French reserves.

Farther north, the attacks by Haig's First Army were progressing no better. British shortages of high explosive shells were significantly worse than the French; the British bombardment lasted just forty minutes. Like Tenth Army commander Victor d'Urbal, Haig had his cavalry in reserve, waiting for the chance to exploit a breakthrough. Also like d'Urbal, his infantry advanced very slowly and at high cost. After a few days of frustration, Lord Kitchener drew the conclusion that "we may take it as proved that the lines cannot be forced."[12]

Still, Foch could not bring himself to abandon the offensive, despite the evidence in front of him. He argued that French forces had very nearly achieved the desired breakthrough and that another well-planned offensive would finish the job. He was preparing a renewed offensive in June when he received explicit instructions from Joffre to call the offensive off. French generals, such firm believers in the cult of the offensive before the war, now had to rethink their most cherished assumptions about the nature of war. French politicians, for their part, soon lost confidence in those generals, like Joffre and Foch, who argued that operations like the one at Arras had been worth the losses. More specifically, Arras led to a severe loss of faith in the Joffre-Foch team. Rather than being seen as an opportunity nearly missed, Arras was seen as a disaster that had produced no gain commensurate with French losses. Some French leaders advocated opening other fronts and directing efforts away from the west.

Lack of faith in Joffre and Foch contributed to the creation of an eastern front, near the Greek city of Salonika. French forces there, under the command of General Maurice Sarrail, were to advance through the Balkans, presumably in country more favorable to the offensive than that of eastern France. The British, too, reinforced their efforts in the Middle East and Gallipoli. Foch was appalled. All evidence to the contrary, he continued to believe that a breakthrough on the western front was not only possible, but the shortest route to victory. He, like Joffre, looked upon any reduction of Allied efforts in France as dangerous and wasteful.

To prove his point, he planned to resume offensives around Arras in September. He convinced Wilson, French, and Kitchener that the offensives deserved another attempt. Joffre, less confident of a breakthrough at Arras, had directed that British and French attacks there would occur simultaneously with an offensive led by Castelnau in Champagne. As a sign of the diminution of his faith in Foch, Joffre allocated the bulk of French forces to Castelnau, who had thirty-four divisions and 850 heavy guns to Foch's seventeen divisions and 420 guns.

Foch resumed the offensive on September 25 with no more success than he had had in May and June. Only one division reached the crest of Vimy Ridge itself, and that success was only temporary. Castelnau's attacks in Champagne were no more successful. French losses were 48,000 in Arras and 143,000 in Champagne to combined German losses of 120,000. Haig's British forces planned to use gas to compensate for the continued lack of high explosive shells, but they were unable to do so because of unfavorable weather. They attacked anyway, losing 60,000 men to Germany's 20,000.

Foch and Joffre survived 1915, but not without criticism. The reputations of both men had been severely tarnished. Still, Foch continued to believe that with proper artillery support, infantry assaults were the best course to win the war. Foch was neither blind to the difficulties of the offensive nor was he insensitive to the enormous casualties. Rather, he continued to be caught in the dilemma of how to remove the hated enemy from the sacred soil of France. Blockades, fronts in Eastern Europe, and a negotiated peace were all out of the question for him. If he can be criticized for developing no original ideas on the tactical level in 1915, it must be noted that he was far from being alone in his inability to find a quick, cheap solution.

More important for the long term, 1915 had provided Foch with invaluable experience in managing the Allied coalition through persuasion rather than through formal authority. He had vastly multiplied his contacts in the British and Belgian armies and had learned how to organize and work within the divergent needs of France's coalition partners. These experiences produced indispensable benefits in 1918 (see chapter 6). But those accomplishments still lay in the future. For 1916, France would have to face a new challenge at Verdun. Although Foch played no direct role in the most important battle of the war thus far, Verdun shaped all of his actions and, indirectly, led to his temporary eclipse.

Chapter 4

Verdun, the Somme, and the Frustrations of Modern War

T HE GREATEST BATTLE of the war for France began in February 1916 at the fortified city of Verdun. German Gen. Erich von Falkenhayn, Foch's opponent during the Yser and Ypres Campaigns, had chosen the site as the test place for his new strategy. Recognizing that the defense had become dominant and that frontal assaults, like those at Ypres, were nearly always futile, Falkenhayn developed a diabolical method to use the tactical stalemate to his advantage. He chose a place that he believed the French would defend to the last man. He counted on Joffre to feed division after division into this sector, where the German armies could, in Falkenhayn's words, "bleed the French white" through better battle management and attrition.

Verdun was a mythic place in French and German history. At Verdun in 843, Charlemagne divided his empire into three sections, two of which formed the seeds of the future French and German nations, while the third, Lotharingia or Lorraine, had been fought over ever since. Verdun and its defenses had successfully resisted German invaders both during the French Revolution and the Franco-Prussian War. It had also held out in 1914 and 1915. Falkenhayn therefore knew that Joffre would have no choice but to fight to the end to defend a place with such military and historic significance to the French. The Germans had no interest in capturing the town nor did they seek to break French lines. Instead, Falkenhayn wanted to grind up French units as they entered what became known as the "slaughterhouse" of Verdun. His goal was to destroy French units more efficiently than the French could destroy German units. His was a new kind of warfare, one that did not focus on territorial gains or breakthroughs, but on the careful management of casualties.

Between February and December 1916, the Battle of Verdun took on a life of its own. Costly French counterattacks and grim determination created an expanding battlefield. Falkenhayn's gruesome calculus did not add up because his troops suffered nearly as badly as did the French. By the end of the year, France had suffered 377,000 casualties to the Germans' 337,000 casualties. The battle lines moved fewer than five miles in ten months. Verdun's sacred place in French history had been reaffirmed and the forts surrounding the city were back in French hands, but the unprecedented horrors and carnage of the campaign marked France indelibly.

Ferdinand Foch did not serve at Verdun. Still, the battle affected everything that Foch did during 1916. Indeed, Foch became a casualty of Verdun, as did Joffre and a whole generation of French generals. By the end of the year, both men had been relieved from command of French soldiers and it appeared yet again that Foch's career was on the verge of ending. For most of the early part of 1917, a new generation of French commanders directed war efforts, leaving Foch frustrated and in charge of marginally important projects.

Foch had developed grandiose plans for 1916. He had planned a major offensive to take place in conjunction with the BEF around the Somme River, where British and French lines converged. Believing still that the offensive at Arras had been a near-success, he planned a much larger and much more ambitious version of the same basic operational plan. As he had done at Arras, he planned a massive artillery bombardment of German lines to be followed by a joint Franco-British infantry assault. The plan reflected his continued belief that properly prepared and well-led offensives were not only possible, but the fastest route to victory.

Foch's view on war had changed somewhat since 1914, but his fundamental belief in the importance of the offensive had not. He had come to understand that frontal assaults were far too costly and that only prodigious use of artillery could reduce French casualties. In late January 1916, he wrote that victory would come from "a series of successive acts, each one necessitating a great deal of artillery and very little infantry."[1] He and BEF commander Sir Douglas Haig planned a mid-summer offensive that would involve forty French divisions and twenty-five British divisions. The French front would be the main operation, covering twenty-five miles.

Verdun destroyed both the timetable and the careful planning for Foch's grand offensive. Joffre soon demanded that the Somme offensive be conducted considerably earlier than originally planned in the hopes of relieving the pressure on Verdun. He also took division after division away from Foch's army group to meet the urgent demands there. Foch's army was reduced from its original forty divisions to thirty divisions and eventually to just sixteen. His twenty-five-mile front had been reduced to just eight. This reduction, with accompanying reductions in the critical heavy guns and ammunition, required Foch to turn over command of the Somme operation to the British under Sir Douglas Haig. His relations with Haig were cordial, but Foch thought him far too cautious and not sufficiently expert in artillery for the type of operation Foch had in mind. Haig for his part thought the Somme terrain, with Germans dug in heavily on the high ground, an unsuitable place for an offensive. Winston Churchill agreed, calling the Somme region "undoubtedly the strongest and most perfectly defended position in the world."[2]

Whatever the challenge, Foch was incapable of sitting idle while the entire war was in the course of being decided at Verdun.

He grew frustrated at his lack of activity, writing in May that "[w]e have done everything and completely succeeded in preventing disaster [at Verdun], but we have done nothing to achieve victory. . . . What would Napoleon say if he saw us buried in our trenches without doing anything!"[3] His desire for action was such that it misled Foch into believing, his recent experiences notwithstanding, that an offensive operation could succeed. Not everyone agreed. One of his subordinate generals, Marie Emile Fayolle, disliked Foch's desire to assume the offensive under such disadvantageous circumstances; he noted in his journal: "Foch came to show us his plan. He has no intention of maneuvering. The battle he dreams of has no goal. . . . 'The German is tapped out' he says. He has repeated it since the beginning of the war. . . . For him, the troops are always ready to attack indefinitely."[4]

Foch must have had private reservations that he did not share with Fayolle, for by the time the date for the Somme Campaign had been set, even he had grown pessimistic about its success. In May he had confided to Weygand, "To aim so large with the means given to us will be to condemn us to great and useless sacrifices."[5] His great French campaign had become a British campaign under the command of a man who did not fully believe in its ultimate success. Foch's own role had been reduced to that of a supporting army commander. Still, because of the crisis at Verdun, the Somme operation had to go on, whatever the odds against it. Foch told a colleague that the situation at the Somme seemed impossible, but that in war it was sometimes necessary to do the impossible.[6]

The task at the Somme was indeed impossible. On July 1, 1916, British troops attacked after a one-week bombardment involving more than a million and half shells. The Germans survived the bombing, which used too many shrapnel shells and not enough high explosive. The German positions, therefore, had not been sufficiently damaged. The British Army lost 60,000 men on the first day of the battle. Of that number, 20,000 were dead. It was the worst single day in the history of the British Army, a dubious distinction that it holds to this day.

Foch's operations had been slightly more successful than Haig's, but without a British breakthrough, they could not achieve significant success of their own.

Falkenhayn did redirect forces away from Verdun, but the Somme Campaign dragged on with little tangible gain to show for all the losses. The battle raged into November, costing the British 420,000 men, the French 195,000 men, and the Germans 465,000 men. Despite all the losses, the lines did not move more than eight miles at any one point. Strong German positions remained in place on the high ground. Haig's anachronistic cavalry attacks dissolved in the face of withering German machine gun fire. Premature attempts to introduce the tank proved to be a failure as well, as twenty-four of the forty-nine machines broke down or otherwise failed to advance.

As in Lorraine in 1914, Foch's troops had advanced the farthest. French troops continued to press forward until mid-July. As late as October, the London media was praising Foch as "a great leader of men" and "the first authority in France on the theory of war."[7] Several possible explanations emerged for why French troops, but not British troops, had achieved limited success. British officers argued that French forces faced easier terrain and less experienced German units, but British Prime Minister David Lloyd George believed otherwise. He shared the conclusion of most French officers that the difference was primarily due to the decisions of the commanders. Lloyd George came to France personally to ask Foch why he had been able to advance while Haig had not. Foch, who knew of Lloyd George's intense dislike and mistrust of Haig, refused to give the prime minister any ammunition he could use to press for Haig's removal. As he had done with Sir John French in 1914 and 1915, Foch secured the personal and professional loyalty of a colleague. This loyalty paid important dividends in the future.

For the immediate moment, however, the French and British governments had to figure out what to do in the aftermath of two horrific campaigns. Both armies had been badly bloodied and had nothing substantive to show in return. Incredibly, Foch proposed more offensives to change the momentum of the war and to head off future German attacks. He believed that the offensives at the Somme had diverted German attention away from Verdun, thereby permitting France to hold onto the city. The French government, then in the process of considering drastic changes, was appalled at Foch's logic. French Prime Minister René Viviani wanted to remove both Joffre and Foch. Foch had reached the mandatory retirement age of sixty-five during the Somme Campaign. While it would have been a simple and routine step to waive the age limit, Viviani wanted to use Foch's age and allegations of ill health to remove him. Joffre, seeing that his own job was in jeopardy, declined to put himself on the line for Foch.

Foch found out from a friend that he was to be removed from his post on grounds of ill health. Enraged, he told the war minister, "I want to kill Boches. If the government wants to recall me from my command, let it do so; but it shall not say that I'm ill for that's a lie!"[8] Foch had in fact been suffering from some health problems, probably related to his bladder or prostate, but it is unlikely that these problems were severe enough to keep him from performing his job. More to the point, the French government had grown tired of the aggressive offensive spirit that had cost so many French casualties for so little gain. After considering a protest to President Poincaré, Foch accepted his fate and, true to form, volunteered to accept command of an infantry division, saying, "It is never a downfall to command French soldiers."[9] His offer was refused. Viviani and the French Parliament had heard enough for now.

Verdun and the Somme had been twin disasters that left the French government demanding a change in commanders. Joffre, too, was soon removed, on the grounds that he had failed to foresee adequately the German attack on Verdun. His acrimonious relationship with Parliament played a considerable role as well. To ease public opinion and to make an outward show of unity, Joffre was promoted to marshal and sent to the United States on a tour to boost American support for the Allied cause. The Joffre-Foch team was now out, to be replaced by the heroes of Verdun, including the choice of most parliamentarians, the effusive and charming Robert Nivelle, and the troops' favorite, Henri Philippe Pétain.

Foch was more sad than angry at his removal. He had been "exiled" once before and, as he had done then, he refused offers of help from sympathetic colleagues and politicians. Recalling that exile, he took the opportunity to get some much-needed rest and to visit his family. Viviani may have grown tired of Foch's spirit, but he recognized Foch's intelligence and gave him a variety of assignments, including the responsibility for drawing up a contingency plan to be used in the event of a German invasion of Switzerland and temporary command of the Seventh and Eighth Armies while their commander, Edouard-Noël de Castelnau, undertook a two-month trip to Russia. Foch saw these assignments as little more than busy work, but he devoted his usual energy to them. He continued to put his faith in the western front, arguing for the removal of French troops from the Salonika front in Greece. He also opposed proposals for operations in Syria, which many politicians wanted to add to the French empire after the war.

Foch had to sit on the sidelines while the French and British armies agreed to Robert Nivelle's plan for a renewed offensive for April 1917. Nivelle had convinced the French and British governments that he had the "formula" to break the stalemate. He proposed a massive preliminary bombardment of German lines to be followed by a "creeping barrage" that would silence German machine guns. Foch believed that the plan looked too much like Haig's at the Somme and predicted that it would end in disaster. There was a cruel irony in Viviani removing Foch from command because he held too closely to the offensive and then agreeing to Nivelle's risky plan. Nivelle, however, had used the creeping barrage tactic effectively near Verdun, albeit on a smaller scale. He had also charmed several politicians, including Lloyd George, who admired Nivelle's fluency in English (learned from his English mother) and saw a chance to subordinate Haig to a commander in whom he had more confidence.

Nivelle's offensive, aimed at the Chemin des Dames ridge, began on April 16, 1917. The French had prepared the ground with more than 11 million shells over a thirty-mile front. But the terrain was unfavorable, and Nivelle and his boastful staff had revealed too many important details of the plan. The Germans, who had air superiority and could thus monitor French movements, were not surprised and moved several units back to prepared defensive positions. As Foch had predicted, the plan mirrored that of the Somme too closely and it failed miserably. Moreover, Nivelle did not honor promises to abandon the offensive if a breakthrough did not materialize within forty-eight hours. Instead, he continued to order repeated direct attacks on German positions. The offensive continued until May 9, costing France 120,000 casualties that it could not afford. On May 15, Nivelle resigned in favor of Pétain.

Upon taking command, Pétain had to face a new problem: disobedience in the ranks. The Nivelle Offensives had been too much, even for the brave French soldiers who had survived Verdun. More than half of the units in the French army refused to attack, and more than 20,000 men deserted. Pétain took immediate action, executing as many as fifty-five ringleaders, but treating the rest of the French army with an even-handed justice that quickly calmed the situation and averted a further disaster. Pétain understood that the men were not acting out of a lack of patriotism. Almost without exception, they were willing to defend their positions, but they were not willing to conduct further offensives that they saw as utterly futile. To address the soldiers' most immediate concerns, Pétain introduced regular leave, ordered the creation of better facilities at the front, and improved food and sleeping quarters. To address their more fundamental concerns, he promised that he would end the suicidal offensives that had cost France so dearly. The American entry into the war in April would produce fresh divisions in 1918, and Pétain was willing to wait on the defensive until they arrived.

Although Foch had predicted the disaster at the Chemin des Dames, the scale of the losses came as a great shock. The mutinies, about which he did not learn until his return from a trip to the Italian front, were a terrifying portent for the future. He blamed the change in commanders from Joffre to Nivelle, arguing that if Joffre had been in command, no mutinies would have occurred. He thus returned to France to find a very different situation from the one he had left, but he was in no position to affect it directly.

France was once again facing a major crisis, and the new prime minister, Paul Painlevé wanted Foch returned to a central role. Remarkably, word of the mutinies had not reached the German commander, Erich Ludendorff, but it was only a matter of time before the Germans discovered the crisis in the French lines and attacked. Painlevé had long been an admirer of Foch's abilities, and on May 15, the same day Pétain replaced Nivelle, Foch was named chief of staff of the French Army. Nevertheless, Foch's ardor for the offensive made many French politicians uneasy. The more cautious Pétain was therefore to have strategic and operational control of the French armies, while Foch was to serve as a technical adviser to the government, an ambiguous role that gave him great influence, but no command authority.

Foch at once recognized the dire situation in the French army. Even he could see that the army was in no condition to conduct offensive operations. He immediately agreed with Pétain's decision to await the arrival of the Americans before resuming a general offensive. Foch's most urgent tasks were therefore to prepare for offensives in 1918 and to plan for the eventual buildup and assimilation of an American army in France. He began to oversee the acquisition of large stockpiles of airplanes, artillery, tanks, and gas. These actions show how far Foch had come from his 1914 belief in the supremacy of élan alone, an idea he later called "infantile." Foch also began to plan for the possibility of a Russian collapse which, by July, appeared increasingly likely and occupied more and more of his time. He developed a plan for sending American and Japanese troops to Siberia to aid the faltering Russians against both the Germans and domestic revolutionaries, but his plan was shelved when the American and Japanese governments showed little interest.

The entry of the Americans and the increasing weakness of the Russians underscored the global nature of the war. Ideas therefore began to circulate about the creation of a central command structure to deal with all Allied operations. In August, Painlevé formally proposed the appointment of Foch as generalissimo of Allied armies. In Painlevé's mind, Foch's experiences in Flanders and at the Somme made him an ideal candidate because he had substantial experience with joint operations. Such an appointment would also play to Foch's great strengths: diplomacy and inter-Allied cooperation. Moreover, since he would be more of a facilitator than a field commander, his offensive tendencies could be tempered. Foch, whose career seemed all but over at the beginning of the year, was now on the verge of assuming overall command of Allied armies.

Painlevé proposed the idea to British Prime Minister David Lloyd George, who warmed to it immediately. As noted above, he had a deep mistrust of Haig, but could not remove him because of the general's impressive political connections. Haig was closely linked with several Conservative members of Lloyd George's coalition government, and he maintained a personal correspondence with King George V. Lloyd George admired Foch and saw the generalissimo plan as a way to subordinate Haig without dismissing him. In a similar vein, Foch had directed operations in Flanders in 1915 as British confidence in Sir John French waned. Lloyd George wanted to repeat the formula in 1917.

Haig and his political allies immediately objected. They were naturally wary of placing British troops under the command of another nation's general, as Foch would have likely objected to placing Frenchmen under English command. The British generals also pointed out (correctly) that Lloyd George had subordinated Haig to Nivelle in April with disastrous consequences. Nor were they as impressed as Lloyd George was with how the arrangements in Flanders had functioned. The Italians also objected, as did the Americans, who insisted on entering the war as

Foch on an official state visit to Great Britain in 1912. British
Secretary of State for War J. E. B. Seeley is at left.
Collection SHAA

A confident Foch poses as commander of the elite Twentieth Corps, 1914.
Collection SHAA

Postcard from 1914 showing the Allied senior generals. Foch is in the back, third from the right. By the end of the war, only Foch, Franchet (fourth from the left), and Castelnau (far right) still held field commands.
Collection SHAA

Foch after the First Battle of the Marne in 1914. He is wearing the
Legion of Honor medal awarded to him after the battle.
Collection SHAA

Foch (right) with Field Marshal Sir John French. Foch spent much of the end of 1914 and 1915 bolstering the confidence of the BEF commander.
Collection SHAA

Fresco by Lucien Jonas in the town hall of Doullens commemorating
the agreement that gave Foch authority to "coordinate the actions of
the allied armies."
Donald Seablom

Foch (left) with John Pershing, commander of the AEF at the latter's
Chaumont Headquarters.
Collection SHAA

Fighting during the Second Battle of the Marne in 1918. At Foch's direction, the Allied armies began the counterattack that eventually led to victory.
National Archives

Ypres — Ruines Eglise St-Martin   Ruins   St-Martin's church.

Destruction of the city of Ypres. Devastation like that at Ypres convinced Foch that Germany was a dangerous and implacable enemy.

National Archives

Foch (second from right) entering Strasbourg in November 1918.
Castelnau is second from the left.
Collection SHAA

Foch leaving the Foreign Office in London after a meeting in December 1918. General Weygand is behind him.
Collection SHAA

"The Big Four": Britain's David Lloyd George, Italy's Vittorio Orlando, France's Georges Clemenceau, and America's Woodrow Wilson. Together they blocked Foch's plan for a separate Rhineland.
National Archives

Foch arriving at the Trianon Palace to present the Versailles terms to the German delegation, 1919. *Collection SHAA*

Believing that the Versailles Treaty did not guarantee French security, Foch refused to attend the formal signing ceremony, seen here.
National Archives

Statue of Foch near the Trocadéro in Paris. The statue looks across the Seine River and the Champ de Mars to a similar statue of Joffre in front of the École Militaire.
Donald Seablom

Foch's tomb in Les Invalides, Paris.
Donald Seablom

an "associated power" rather than an ally. The idea therefore faded, but did not entirely disappear.

In October, the idea of a single command took on new urgency with the Austro-German attack against the Italians at Caporetto. After eleven inconclusive battles along the Isonzo River, the Austrians and Germans finally succeeded in breaking the Italian line and routing the Italian Second Army. The Germans and Austrians used new "Hutier" (also known as "storm troop") tactics to gain local numerical supremacy despite having an overall deficiency in divisions in the Italian theater of thirty-five to forty-one. Italian morale quickly evaporated as units fled from the field. The Italian Third Army, left exposed by the rout of the Second, also retreated. Total Italian losses included 265,000 prisoners and 300,000 deserters. Italy seemed on the verge of being eliminated as an Allied power.

Foch, who had been to Italy in April, had an important first-hand understanding of the situation there. He set off immediately upon hearing of the Second Army collapse. Within a week after the beginning of the Caporetto Offensive, Foch was in Italy meeting with King Victor Emmanuel III and the new Italian Prime Minister, Vittorio Orlando. He found Orlando anxious to replace Gen. Luigi Cadorna with Gen. Armando Diaz who, like Pétain, was popular with his men. Also like Pétain, Diaz worked to improve the daily conditions of his men, thus raising their morale and keeping them from deserting. Foch, who found Cadorna disoriented and confused by the Caporetto breakthrough, agreed.

To stem the immediate disaster, Foch worked with Diaz to stop the Italian retreat and to establish a defensive line on the Piave River, just twenty miles north of Venice. Foch then arranged for General Fayolle, his subordinate during the Somme campaign, to bring six French divisions to Italy. He also convinced Haig to send Gen. Hubert Plumer with an additional five British divisions. Thus reinforced, the Italians were able to regroup and hold onto the area near Venice. Italy had been rescued, and the disaster at Caporetto had awakened the Italians to the need to renew their efforts on the battlefield. Foch's work during his first visit to Italy in April, combined with his aggressive actions in October, helped to keep the Italians in the war.

The near-catastrophe at Caporetto had also convinced Painlevé to renew his efforts to create a supreme command. Acting on Lloyd George's suggestion, the Allies hurriedly called for a conference at the Italian city of Rapallo, near Genoa, on November 5 and 6. Foch continued to favor the creation of a single Allied commander, similar to the generalissimo idea that had surfaced in the summer. The British remained disinclined to accept a single general in command, so the Allies reached a compromise.

In place of a generalissimo, the Allies created a Supreme War Council, based at Versailles, to be composed of one head of state, one cabinet member, and one senior military officer from each nation. Foch instantly disliked the idea of command by committee, but agreed to serve as France's military representative. He also disliked the makeup of the Council because politicians outnumbered generals by a margin of two to one. He was, however, pleased to learn that his old friend Sir Henry Wilson would represent Britain. The Americans sent Gen. Tasker Bliss to sit as their representative to the council and to begin the coordination necessary to land sizable American forces the following spring. Foch left Rapallo believing that the Allies had made a small step toward the creation of a supreme command, but that the creation of a system of command by committee posed significant dangers. He believed that the Rapallo system addressed political expediency more than military necessity.

Foch remained in Italy two more weeks, overseeing the preparation of Allied lines along the Piave River and arranging a transition of authority in Italy from himself to Fayolle. He returned to France on November 23 to find, much to his surprise, that the Painlevé government, which had just recently finalized the Rapallo agreement, had fallen. Georges Clemenceau was now prime minister and, as his predecessor had done, he had also assumed the war ministry portfolio. "The Tiger," as Clemenceau was often called, was back, and he quickly imposed his dominating personality on the situation at hand. Clemenceau instantly disliked the idea of the Supreme War Council; he believed it was a threat to his authority as head of the French government. He also had an innate distrust of generals, partly as a holdover from his days as Alfred Dreyfus's most vocal defender. But Clemenceau was first and foremost a patriot. He was the last survivor of the 1871 National Assembly that had witnessed the humiliation of the Treaty of Frankfurt. Like Foch, he was determined to see the war through to a successful conclusion, whatever the cost.

By the end of 1917, the situation looked increasingly grim. Rumania had been beaten and Italy was still in the war only by virtue of the eleven French and British divisions that had to be moved out of the western front. More ominously, Russia's collapse would soon permit Germany to redirect significant resources from the eastern to the western front. By March 1918, the Germans had 192 divisions, all under a unified command, on the western front to oppose 170 Allied divisions under six different commands. Only the promised arrival of the Americans could even the balance sheet for 1918. Any intelligent observer of the situation could predict that the Germans would assume the offensive early in 1918, using the transfers from the Russian front to gain the upper hand before the arrival of hundreds of thousands of Americans. As 1917 became 1918, Foch knew that defeating that offensive might very well decide the fate of the war and the future of France.

Chapter 5

Becoming Generalissimo

THROUGHOUT THE WINTER of 1917–18, Ferdinand Foch considered the problem of meeting the expected German offensive. Although he preferred a preemptive Allied offensive, several barriers stood in his way. Most important, Haig and Pétain, the British and French commanders-in-chief, respectively, were at that point considering only defensive operations. The Somme, Verdun, and the Nivelle Offensives left the French Army too weak for Pétain to consider any sustained offensives. Foch may have done so, but, under the terms of the Rapallo agreement, it was Pétain's decision and he decided to remain on the defensive until the arrival en masse of the Americans.

Partly because of his own failures, Haig's mindset was similar to Pétain's. The British Army had been severely weakened by a disastrous British offensive in the Ypres salient near the town of Passchendaele from July to November. Haig's ambitious plan to drive deep into Belgium literally drowned in the torrential rains and mud of Flanders. The offensive cost the British 240,000 men to move the lines fewer than five miles. The Americans on whom Pétain counted were not yet prepared to send trained units in large numbers, so, Foch's desires notwithstanding, the Allies had no troops with which to conduct major offensive operations.

Failing a preemptive offensive, Foch argued for three steps to stop the Germans and buy time for the Americans to arrive in force. First, he argued for a complete dedication of Allied forces to the western front. He successfully blocked a plan by Lloyd George and Sir Henry Wilson to redirect Allied efforts to the east against Turkey. Foch saw no militarily sound reason to denude the western front of troops at the very moment that a German attack on France seemed imminent. He had always been a confirmed "westerner" and had to contend constantly with the wishes of those "easterners" who sought decisive action in the Balkans or the Middle East.

Second, he wanted to create a general reserve of men from all the Allied nations, capable of responding to a crisis at any point along the line. Foch argued that since the Allies could guess at the timing of the German offensive but not its target (or targets), it made sense to have a reserve of men prepared to fill gaps and conduct counteroffensives. The British feared that the main weight of the German attack would come against them in Flanders, while most French commanders assumed that the main weight would come against French forces in Champagne. A mobile general reserve could meet either or both eventualities. In his first proposal for a general reserve in January 1918, Foch suggested a force of thirteen French divisions, ten British divisions, and seven Italian divisions. The Americans would eventually be expected to contribute as well. On February 6, the Supreme War Council approved Foch's formula in principle.

Finally, Foch argued that the reserve, and the western front more generally, needed a single commander. Foch offered as proof his contention that the only limited gains at the Somme had occurred when the British and French had coordinated their attacks. "The entire front," he argued, "must be considered as a whole, not the French as one part and the British as another."[1] Foch often quoted Napoleon's maxim, "One bad general is better than two good ones." That general would be charged with directing the reserve to trouble spots, then determining the timing and nature of the counterstrikes. The job would require a soldier's vision with a diplomat's tact. It did not take long for all members of the Supreme War Council to see that Foch had himself in mind for the job.

Still, Foch's voice was only one on the Council and power struggles soon ensued, between the British and French on the one hand, and between politicians and generals on the other. Clemenceau and Lloyd George insisted that, as elected heads of their respective governments, the Council was their body and the soldiers were there to provide "technical advice" only. Once when Foch began to respond to a comment from Lloyd George, Clemenceau leaned toward him and said, "Be quiet. I am the representative of France."[2] Both prime ministers had a healthy suspicion of generals and determined to use the Council to dilute their authority. The Council debates foreshadowed intense arguments between Foch and Clemenceau during the Paris Peace Conference (see chapter 7).

Nor were the soldiers in full agreement with one another. The British generals, led by Haig, strenuously opposed the general reserve concept. At a Council meeting on March 4, Haig threatened to resign rather than see British units transferred to the reserve. His opposition was based primarily on his unwillingness to see British troops under the command of a foreign general. As a result, the reserve, even as a theoretical concept, collapsed. On March 14, Haig renewed his criticism of the general reserve and, to Foch's dismay, Clemenceau switched sides and backed Haig. Foch had intelligence reports indicating that the offensive was just weeks, or even days, away. Without a reserve, there was no way to execute a coordinated defense or conduct coordinated counteroffensives.

Foch's intelligence reports were correct. Gen. Erich Ludendorff's great German Spring Offensives of 1918 began on March 21. Using the same storm troop tactics that had produced the breakthrough at Caporetto, the Germans attacked toward the critical juncture of the French and British armies at Amiens. These tactics involved the use of gas instead of artillery to pin down the frontline Allied defenders. Then, specially trained soldiers moved to the enemy rear to disrupt communications and inhibit the arrival of reinforcements. Finally, infantry reserves moved forward to disable the now-isolated frontline positions. The tactics worked very well in the initial stages, routing many Allied units and gaining 1,200 square miles in two weeks. Mobility returned to the battlefield, and the war took on an entirely different character.

The initial success of the German offensives created a near-panic at the Supreme War Council. In Paris, the French government began preparations to make another evacuation to Bordeaux. On the second day of the offensive, the Germans crossed the Somme River without having to fire a shot. To the British, who had lost so many men in 1916 trying to cross the same river, the German advance came as a great shock. British generals began to speak again about retreating toward the Channel ports, a movement that would have opened up a huge gap between the British and French lines.

A British retreat to the north was Foch's worst nightmare. If they did so, the French would be obliged to turn south in an effort to protect Paris, opening a gap near the city of Amiens where British and French lines converged. The Allied armies would then be too far apart from one another to offer mutual support. The Germans could then move into the opening and outflank the British from the south and the French from the north. With no general reserve to plug the gap and no unified commander to direct Allied responses, the Germans would have a golden opportunity to defeat one ally, then turn on the other, and march unopposed into Paris.

With the situation looking increasingly dire, the Council called for an emergency meeting on March 26 at the city hall of Doullens, the seat of Foch's headquarters for a time in 1914. As they arrived, the conferees could hear the sound of artillery fire nearby. Given the crisis, Foch expected that the British would have little choice but to accept a single commander in exchange for promises of French reserves to reinforce their right wing. Clemenceau was initially in favor of giving the job to Pétain, but when Pétain arrived at Doullens, he was despondent and utterly pessimistic of the chances of ultimate victory. He told Clemenceau, "The Germans will defeat the English in open country, after which they will defeat us."[3] Clemenceau was shocked ("should a general talk, or even think, like that?" he asked) and immediately decided against Pétain. Foch, on the other hand, arrived full of energy and "ready to throw himself bodily into the battle and to assume the heavy responsibility of the strategic direction, and that because he felt within him the soul of a great leader."[4]

The meeting quickly became Foch's stage. When Pétain urged the evacuation of Paris, Foch screamed: "Paris has nothing to do with it! Paris is a long way off! It is where we now stand that the enemy will be stopped!"[5] Clemenceau was reinvigorated by Foch's indomitable confidence. He then turned to him and asked for his thoughts on the current situation. Foch replied:

Oh, my plan is not complicated. I would fight without a break. I would fight in front of Amiens. I would fight in Amiens. I would fight behind Amiens. I would fight all the time, and, by force of hitting, I would finish by shaking up the Boche; he's neither cleverer nor stronger than we are. In any case, for the moment it is as in 1914 on the Marne; we must dig in and die where we stand if need be; to withdraw a foot will be an act of treason.[6]

The sermon moved Clemenceau as well as Haig, who told the French prime minister that he could accept Foch as generalissimo. Lloyd George, recalling Foch's ability to save the British Army once before in Flanders, concurred, saying that Foch "inspires in all the Allies a full confidence."[7]

The Council quickly drafted a memorandum that authorized Foch to "coordinate the action of the Allied armies" on the western front. Haig, to the surprise of many at Doullens, had been Foch's strongest supporter, extending his powers beyond the original draft written by Clemenceau. With the British Army in serious jeopardy, he counted on Foch to override Pétain's gloomy caution and dispatch French reserves to the Amiens sector immediately. Within minutes, Foch was bent over a map with Pétain and could be heard shouting: "No question of that! . . . It's not possible. . . . We shall stop them. . . . Give the order. . . . We shan't retire any further."[8]

Later that day, Clemenceau turned to Foch and said, "Well, you've got it at last, your high command." Foch quickly retorted, "It's a fine present you've made me; you give me a lost battle and tell me to win it."[9] Exactly how he was supposed to win it remained unclear. He had been given only vague powers to "coordinate" Allied actions. He had no authority to command and he still had no general reserve. By the following morning, Foch had set up a small staff in the city hall of the town of Beauvais, with Maxime Weygand as its most important member. Foch and Weygand guessed that the Germans would fight two battles: first, operations around Amiens to drive a wedge between the French and British armies and, second, operations along the Channel ports to cut off Allied reinforcements. Foch's thinking, even at this point, centered on the quest for the Clausewitzian culminating point, or the point at which the German offensives lost momentum and the Allies could themselves resume the offensive.

The Doullens agreement left considerable room for confusion. Foch had overall strategic control of the Allied armies, but King Albert I of Belgium, Pétain, Haig, and Diaz remained commanders-in-chief of their own national armies. Foch therefore urged more than ordered Pétain and Haig to converge on Amiens to prevent a gap from opening there. He had to convince Pétain, who wanted to retreat, to keep fighting for Amiens. He also had to convince Haig that massing near Amiens did not mean that he intended to abandon the critical Channel ports. Foch was operating on familiar ground. As he had done in Flanders earlier in the war, he acted through persuasion rather than coercion and used his infectious spirit and energy to carry through his vision. The American decision on March 28 to contribute to the strategic reserve gave the idea new momentum and Foch took steps toward its creation. After a few days of studying the situation, Foch calmly told the Council, "I've seen what there is to see, done what there is to do. I can stop them."[10]

Confidence in Foch was rising, leading the Council to amend the Doullens agreement both to specify more clearly what Foch's responsibilities would be and to allow Foch to direct counteroffensives, a power not specified at Doullens. Accordingly, the Supreme War Council met again at Foch's Beauvais headquarters on April 3. The new agreement, signed by the United States, Britain, and France, gave Foch more power, but it was every bit as carefully worded as the Doullens agreement it replaced. The Beauvais agreement gave Foch "strategic direction of military operations," but allowed each national commander to appeal any of Foch's decisions to his respective government. Italy and Belgium agreed in principle, but did not sign the Beauvais agreement.

Within twenty-four hours of the signing of the Beauvais agreement, Foch had met with every Allied army commander on the western front. His orders to all of them were the same: hold on at all costs and keep contact between the British and French sectors intact. Significantly, Foch did not order counterattacks nor did he reinstitute the bloody standing orders at Verdun that all ground lost must be immediately retaken. He planned to remain on the defensive until the opportunity to attack presented itself.

Foch had to use all of his powers of persuasion to keep Haig from retreating to the Channel ports when the second major German offensive struck Flanders in mid-April. The two commanders met sixty times between April and the end of the war. Foch deployed ten divisions of French reinforcements to Flanders out of the strategic reserve and overrode Haig's order to abandon and destroy Dunkirk. During desperate fighting in April and May, the British Army lost nearly 300,000 men. To aid the suffering British, Foch ordered Pétain to assume seventy-five more miles of the western front to shorten the British area of operations. Still, he refused to permit the British to fall back on the Channel ports. Neither would he permit Henry Wilson to order the opening of the sluice gates as the Allies had done in Flanders in 1914. To do so might slow the counteroffensives he planned to conduct in the near future.

Foch's next challenge was the Americans. In late March, John Pershing, in his imperfect French, had made an extraordinary statement to Foch: "[T]he American people would consider it a great honor for our troops to be engaged in the present battle. . . . Infantry, artillery, aviation, all that we have is yours; use them as you wish."[11] But Pershing's ardor, however admirable, could not rapidly increase the number of Americans then available. By the end of April, one year after American entry into the war, the United States had just five divisions (70,000 men) in France.

Foch desperately wanted to increase the flow of American troops. Once in France, he argued, the Yanks could be hurriedly trained or thrown into existing units, but as long as they remained in American training centers, they were of no practical use. The sticking point was on the American side: President Woodrow Wilson and General Pershing wanted to retain as much operational independence as possible for the American Expeditionary Force (AEF). Thus they insisted on sending only fully formed and trained units to France.

The Americans also adamantly refused to see their companies and regiments absorbed into European divisions. This debate over the "amalgamation" of American troops long remained a point of intense disagreement. The Europeans, desperate for men, argued that the Americans could best be used to make up manpower shortfalls in existing units. There they could learn about modern warfare firsthand from troops who had been fighting it. The Americans, with images of Verdun and Passchendaele fresh in their mind, were horrified. Moreover, President Wilson wanted to be sure that the Americans made a separate and clearly identifiable contribution to victory in order to strengthen his hand at the postwar peace negotiations. Shortly after his dramatic offer to Foch, Pershing told Foch that he was willing to risk the Allies being driven back to the Loire River rather than accept amalgamation. The Americans, he told Foch, could exist under Foch's "overall strategic direction," but they would fight as American units under American officers or not at all.

Foch feared that by the time the Americans, with their inexperience and deficiencies in shipping, assembled and prepared an army, the Allies might very well have their backs on the Loire. Augmented by transfers from the Russian front, the Germans had numerical superiority on the western front. Without the Americans, there was no way to counter the operational flexibility that superior numbers gave to the Germans. In late April, when Foch met with Pershing and American representative to the Supreme War Council Gen. Tasker Bliss, he convinced them of the necessity of getting Americans to France as quickly as possible and working out specific arrangements for their use later.

After meeting with British representatives at the Supreme War Council, Foch negotiated the Abbeville agreement, signed on May 2. The Americans promised to send six divisions to France immediately and send only infantry in May and June. The British donated the needed shipping to move the infantry, while the Americans agreed to use their own ships to move cavalry, artillery, and support personnel as they became available. The agreement meant that Foch could expect at least 450,000 American troops—although most of them were only rudimentarily trained—in France by July and a million Americans by the end of the year.

Foch then turned to plans to resume the offensive in Flanders and around Amiens. Once again, the Germans beat him to the punch, launching their third offensive of 1918 on May 27. With thirty divisions, the Germans crossed the Chemin des Dames, the scene of Nivelle's disastrous offensive the year before, and began to push toward the Marne River. Pétain begged for the return of the French reserves that Foch had sent to Flanders, but Foch refused, characteristically issuing an order for a "foot by foot" defense and forbidding both retreats and the construction of elastic defensive lines. But forbidding retreats did not keep them from occurring, especially in the face of overwhelming

German onslaughts. On May 30, Foch ordered the five existing American divisions to a quiet sector to the south to free up French soldiers to come north. He also ordered Haig to stretch his line south to offer support to the French Sixth Army. Haig did not care for the order, but, respecting the Beauvais agreement, he obeyed it. The Allies were bending, but, thanks to Foch, they were not breaking.

Nevertheless, the German success at the Chemin des Dames led to a call in the French Chamber of Deputies for Foch to be replaced, with Pétain emerging as the leading candidate. Little did the deputies know that the retreats were partly the result of Pétain's own pessimism. On May 30, the tide in the Chamber seemed to be rising against Foch. Clemenceau, though he did not fully understand Foch's actions, trusted Foch's spirit and patriotism. He surely understood, as most deputies did not, that Pétain was subject to potentially fatal bouts of defeatism, a tendency that (twenty-two years later) would cost France dearly. Clemenceau went to the Chamber on June 4 and delivered a speech in which he announced his full support for Foch. He made it clear that the choice was not between Foch and Pétain. France, in his view, had to stand with both: "Foch and Pétain are right now waging the most difficult battle of the war and they are waging it with a heroism that leaves me unable to find a worthy expression. . . . The French people have done all that they are capable of doing. . . . It remains for the living to finish the magnificent work of the dead."[12]

Clemenceau had also signaled privately that he would resign if the Chamber voted to remove Foch. Foch survived the Chamber vote by a comfortable margin of 377 to 110. Clemenceau, the rabid anticlerical, had placed his own political career on the line for Foch, the devout Catholic. It was the high point of their relationship.

Thanks to Clemenceau, Foch's job was secure, but the chaos of the western front continued into June as the Germans launched a fourth offensive south toward the Oise River between the towns of Mondidier and Noyon. Through it all, Foch remained calm, confident, and absolutely unshaken in his belief that the tide would soon turn. He inspired both amazement and bewilderment by talking of *when* the Allies would resume the offensive, even as they were then in the process of retreating nearly every day. In early May he wrote, "The offensive alone will enable us to bring the battle to a victorious close and, by seizing the initiative, assert our moral ascendancy."[13] In stark contrast to the mood in Paris and London, his headquarters was so calm that it became known as "the monastery," both because of its tranquility and because of the abiding faith of its high priest, who, all evidence to the contrary, adamantly refused to admit the precariousness of the Allied situation. "Materially," Foch said in April, "I do not see that victory is possible. Morally, I am certain that we shall gain it."[14]

Foch was truly meeting his moment and lifting the spirit of his subordinates. When one of them congratulated him on his appointment, he replied, "But it is nothing calling for praise for a soldier to accept responsibility. One does not refuse when it is France!"[15] He had even inspired the cynical Clemenceau, who had grown so enamored of Foch's spirit that he canceled Pétain's right of appeal as called for in the Beauvais agreement. Now that mobility had returned to the battlefield, Foch's offensive mindset was more in line with the nature of the war than it had been in 1915. Conversely, Pétain's caution, so important at Verdun, was out of step with the war of 1918. Clemenceau thus told Pétain to obey Foch thereafter without questioning. Clemenceau still thought Foch was too reckless, but, as he told a colleague, "[H]e puts heart into everybody."[16] Foch thereupon gave Pétain a standing order not to retreat in Lorraine, as he was then planning to do, and he replaced Pétain's chief of staff without consulting him.

With his professional reputation soaring, Foch's salient personality traits began to emerge. Despite the numerous people who vied for his time, he kept largely to himself, possessing a staff so small that it occupied just two rooms. Only his chief of staff, Maxime Weygand, saw him regularly and was permitted into his confidence. He had few distractions or leisure activities, taking breaks from a fifteen-hour workday only to sleep, eat, and pray. He was most often seen leaning over maps or sharing ideas during long walks with Weygand at a barely audible whisper. To most visitors at the monastery, he seemed distant and almost ethereal. René Viviani's description of Foch as a "mystic" was meant to be pejorative; nevertheless, it reveals much of the character of a man who was hard to know and harder still to comprehend.

Isolated as he was and dealing with a situation as tense as that of spring 1918, Foch cared only about victory. Balancing French and British interests proved to be one of his most difficult tasks. Every decision he made appeared to French generals to benefit the British, while those same decisions appeared to British generals to help France. Even his good friend Henry Wilson complained in early July, after the "angriest meeting we have had," that the French were "attempting to confine the conduct of the war in the interests of France alone."[17] When Foch made decisions that accorded with Haig's vision, he and Wilson nevertheless complained that they were not being fully informed of decisions made at the monastery. Foch disliked large meetings and held just two full conferences during the entire spring, relying instead on personal phone calls and one-on-one meetings. Such a system inevitably left important people in the dark about his exact decisions and actions. Foch's thorny situation was made even more tangled by the confused command structure, which impelled him to lead but gave him no formal authority to actually command.

The Allies faced the fifth German offensive of 1918 with the help of the American Second and Third Divisions near Château Thierry. In spite of their inexperience, the Americans were of necessity coming to occupy a more and more important role in the fighting in France. Foch and Pershing were alike in their stubbornness and absolute commitment to the offensive. The stubbornness created many problems between the two men, but a shared preference for the offensive created a basis for common un-

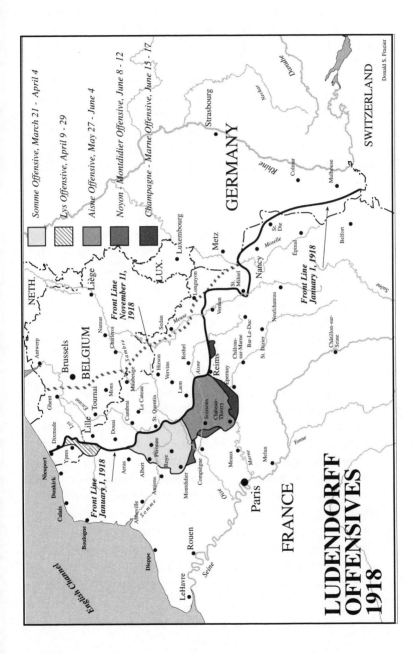

LUDENDORFF
OFFENSIVES
1918

Somme Offensive, March 21 - April 4

Lys Offensive, April 9 - 29

Aisne Offensive, May 27 - June 4

Noyon - Montdidier Offensive, June 8 - 12

Champagne - Marne Offensive, June 15 - 17

Donald S. Frazier

derstanding. Pershing wanted a chance to prove that the Americans could fight. Foch had no choice but to give them that opportunity. Their early successes were a pleasant surprise, and Foch finally agreed to allow the Americans to fight "unamalgamated," that is, under their own flag and officers. On July 10, Foch enthusiastically told Pershing, "Today, when there are a million Americans in France, I am going to be still more American than any of you. . . . The American Army must become an accomplished fact."[18] It proved to be a smart decision, as the men of the AEF made up for their inexperience with an energy and courage that impressed both their allies and their German enemies.

With the end of the fifth German offensive, Foch felt that the tide was turning and that the Allies were approaching the culminating point. He expected a new round of German attacks to commence shortly in both the Marne and Flanders sectors. He knew that the Germans were tiring and he wanted to preempt their offensive with one of his own. Pétain, ever the more cautious of the two, argued in favor of the Napoleonic tactic of allowing the enemy to attack first, then responding with well-directed counters. Foch reluctantly concurred and waited for his chance.

That chance came, as it had in 1914, at the Marne River. Tenth Army commander General Charles "The Butcher" Mangin believed that the Germans were weakening and saw a chance to counterattack. The Americans east of Château Thierry had destroyed the German pontoon bridges across the river, then annihilated the trapped Germans who had arrived to reinforce the sector. Near the town of Nanteuil-Pourcy, Italian troops had thrown back another German attack. Mangin believed that the culminating point was at hand. Pétain, with his usual caution, canceled Mangin's attack. But Foch, sensing the moment, overrode him and ordered Mangin to go forward. A second great battle was about to be fought on the Marne and, like the first, it was to change the course of the war and the fortunes of Ferdinand Foch.

Chapter 6

Winning the War

Ferdinand Foch could have looked back on the events of the first half of 1918 with considerable pride. On the strategic level, he had fused together an effective coalition of French, British, Belgian, American, and Italian armies that now acted in concert. On the operational level, the juncture between the British and French lines near Amiens had held, promising that whatever gains the Germans had managed to achieve, they would eventually be stopped. On the tactical level, the Allies had found ways to respond to their enemy's storm troop tactics. On the political level, he found a modus operandi, albeit a temporary one, with the demanding French prime minister, Georges Clemenceau, who shared Foch's overall aims but remained suspicious of generals and jealous of threats to his own power.

Still, Foch knew that these achievements, impressive though they were, would not win the war by themselves. The Allies had to resume the offensive. The opportunity at the Marne was the best chance of 1918 so far to do so; once it presented itself, Foch did not hesitate. He had been planning to resume the offensive for weeks. Now he believed that his chance was finally at hand.

French intelligence officers expected the Germans to attack the British again in Flanders in the near future. Foch hoped to use an offensive of his own at the Marne to disrupt German planning. He was so determined to attack that he transferred six British divisions south of the Somme River, despite warnings that the Germans were ready to begin their Flanders offensive within days.

In light of the German plans, Foch's offensive was not without risks. If the Germans attacked in Flanders before he could assemble Allied forces on the Marne, they would face a British Army denuded of troops specifically by Foch's order. It was a dangerous gamble, but his decision to overrule Pétain and order Charles Mangin's Tenth Army to attack dramatically changed the course of the war in France. Foch, almost alone among Allied generals, was fully prepared to take the risk necessary to win another great battle on the Marne.

Foch had complete faith in Mangin, probably because he was the only general on the western front who matched Foch's offensive and risk-taking spirit. He was one of the few senior officers who had led charges personally. In 1917, Mangin had been one of the Nivelle Offensive's strongest supporters. When that operation ended in disaster, "The Butcher" lost his command. Not surprisingly, given their shared enthusiasm for attacking, Foch brought him back and assigned him to command the Tenth Army. Mangin was a native of the "lost province" of Lorraine, a background trait that may help to explain his abiding commitment to attacking Germans. He was ready to strike wherever and whenever Foch ordered him to do so.

Mangin would not have to wait much longer. Recently captured German POWs informed the French that the Germans were planning to open another offensive with an attack west of Reims on July 14, Bastille Day. Foch immediately deduced (correctly) that the Reims attack was a diversion for a larger German offensive in Flanders. He ordered preemptive artillery strikes to disrupt the offensive to buy time for his men to get in position for his own offensive, scheduled to begin on July 18. The Germans attacked despite the Allied artillery barrage, pushing back the French Fifth Army and crossing the Marne River. But the Germans of July were clearly not the same Germans that began the Spring Offensives in March. By the time of the Second Battle of the Marne, Ludendorff had just sixty-six total divisions in reserve (many of them seriously depleted), as opposed to the eighty-two full-strength divisions that he had had in reserve in March. With Americans arriving at the rate of 300,000 per month, Ludendorff knew that the Germans could not sustain offensive operations for much longer.

The second phase of Ludendorff's Reims attack struck at the American Third Division, which held firm, giving Foch time to respond. Allied aircraft and artillery pounded the German positions, disrupting supply, damaging bridges, and ultimately causing the attack to lose momentum. The Germans were now left with an exposed salient and the Marne River running through their position. Ludendorff quickly realized the precariousness of his situation and prepared to withdraw to a shorter and more defensible line. Foch, however, had no intention of letting his enemy evacuate the salient without a fight.

Foch finally had the opportunity he had sought for so long. On July 18, Mangin's Tenth Army, which temporarily included the American First and Second Divisions, led the attack. The French Fifth and Sixth French Armies, which included more American divisions, also participated. The immediate goals were to blunt German momentum and capture the railroad juncture of Soissons. On the first day of the attack, French forces reached Soissons and the Allies captured 10,000 German prisoners. By the time the battle ended on August 3, Allied armies had captured 30,000 prisoners, 600 heavy guns, and 3,000 machine guns. The Marne salient no longer existed. The Allies had regained twenty-eight miles of French soil and, with the Paris-to-Soissons rail line reopened, they were in an excellent position to attack east.

Foch at once understood that the Second Battle of the Marne had changed the entire complexion and momentum of the war.

As he had correctly deduced, the Allied attack led Ludendorff to postpone, then cancel, his planned offensive in Flanders. The Germans never took the initiative again. True to the promise Foch made to his wife, Paris was safe. Moreover, the attack vindicated Foch's demands for a general reserve and a unified command. Four French armies, eight American divisions, two Italian divisions, and 300 British tanks contributed to the victory.

The battle represented the first significant Allied victory on the western front since Verdun. Lloyd George called it "the most brilliant counterstroke in the annals of war."[1] Clemenceau was so delighted with the outcome that he recommended to President Poincaré that Foch be promoted to Marshal of France, an honor that was officially bestowed on him in August. The promotion meant that Foch now formally outranked Pershing, and, more significantly, Pétain. The chain of command, especially in the French Army, became much clearer.

Even before the Second Battle of the Marne had ended, Foch was thinking of more grandiose plans. In a memorandum written on July 24, while the battle still raged, he drew the following conclusions: German and Allied manpower were now roughly equal; the German shock armies had been severely weakened; the Allies had air superiority; and German morale was at the breaking point. With the continued arrival of American men, matériel, and money, the situation would only improve. It was, therefore, time to assume the offensive on all fronts and with all possible resources. Foch wanted to regain and resume the initiative with a "series of blows" aimed at keeping the Germans off balance, retaking the Channel ports of Dunkirk and Calais, and opening rail junctures at Amiens and St. Mihiel. When one offensive died down, he would start another, but he would make certain that the pressure on Germany was constant. In another memorandum, written at the same time, Foch revealed what the change of momentum meant to him, both strategically and personally: "We're holding them. We're hitting them in the flank. We're kicking and punching them. We're killing off the enemy. Our dead . . . my son . . . my son-in-law . . . are avenged."[2]

Foch felt that a chance to win the war was approaching. Only his own subordinate commanders threatened to hold him back. Haig and Pétain argued that their own troops were too tired to attack and that the Americans, even with their isolated successes, were still too raw for a general offensive. Lloyd George agreed, and doubted that the Allies could win before 1920. Clemenceau admitted that Allied troops were tired, but he desperately wanted Foch to continue to take the fight to the Germans. He argued that, to do so, the Americans should bear the brunt of the fighting while the French and British armies regrouped.

Foch, however, had no interest in a partial offensive. He told General Fayolle, "We are not going to stop to breathe; we shall, on the contrary, push harder than ever and redouble our efforts." Fayolle, ever cautious with the lives of his men, protested, saying, "But my men are dropping with fatigue." Foch calmly replied, "The Germans are dropping with still more fatigue."[3] Foch stood almost alone in his thinking, but, ever true to his faith in the power of the attack, he continued to push for keeping up the fight in all sectors. "They all took me for a madman," he later wrote.[4]

Madman or prophet, Foch had momentum on his side and a dominating will that carried others with him. He had his eyes clearly set on the area around Amiens, a critical railroad juncture on the Somme River. He argued that behind the withered and exhausted German shock troops stood second-rate troops "condemned to be sacrificed."[5] If he could strike quickly and achieve surprise, he believed that he could win a great victory. Above all, he did not want to give Ludendorff time to reform his troops behind prepared defensive positions to the east. "Having grabbed his enemy by the throat," Weygand later wrote, Foch "did not allow him any respite."[6]

Foch launched the attack on Amiens on August 8, just five days after the fighting at the Marne had ended. As he had hoped, surprise was near-total. Amiens was a joint operation between the British Fourth Army and French First Army. The Germans had grown accustomed to the Allies preceding their assaults with heavy artillery bombardments. At Amiens, the Allies used tank support in lieu of a preliminary artillery bombardment. As the Germans had done with their storm troop tactics, the Allies by-passed many frontline units and moved quickly into the rear. The Germans began to withdraw, only to find that many of their avenues of retreat had been blocked.

Although Foch intuitively understood the magnitude of his victory, he could only have guessed at what a great calamity Amiens seemed to his German enemies. Ludendorff famously called August 8 the "Black Day" of the German Army and con-cluded that, as a result, "The war must be ended!" Germany had lost more than 100,000 men, almost one-third of them prison-ers. The French and British combined had lost 42,000 men, a fa-vorable casualty ratio that they had never known in a battle as large as Amiens. Amiens was a tremendous victory on every level. Foch, elated, began to sense that he might be able to win the war in 1918, not 1919 as Clemenceau thought, or 1920 as Lloyd George pessimistically concluded.

Sensing that the Germans were close to breaking, Foch next set his sights on the St. Mihiel salient, just south of Verdun. He ordered that plans to assault the salient be moved up as rapidly as possible. St. Mihiel sat in the newly created American sector. General Pershing's staff had already drawn up detailed plans for the offensive. Those plans called for seventeen American divi-sions to strike at the northern and southern flanks of the salient simultaneously. Foch had different ideas. He wanted to split the Americans into a First and Second Army and redirect American efforts to a northern attack to be launched west of Verdun toward the Meuse-Argonne sector. Pershing grew alarmed when Foch announced that he intended to place the French Second Army between the two American armies and, more significant, that he planned to transfer six American divisions to French control.

Once again, the ambiguities of the Beauvais agreement caused tension and confusion. Pershing believed that Foch was attempting to minimize both the St. Mihiel offensive and Amer-ica's role in it. At a meeting on August 30, Foch insisted upon his version of the plan, at which point Pershing told him, "I absolutely decline to agree to your plan. While our army will fight wherever you may decide, it will not fight except as an independent American army."[7] Pershing reminded Foch that the Beauvais agreement did not permit him to place Americans under French control without Pershing's explicit approval. He also produced a letter from President Wilson insisting that Pershing not permit the Americans to be divided. Foch abruptly left the meeting without an agreement. The entire offensive now seemed in jeopardy.

True to his nature, Foch resolved the impasse with tact and compromise rather than by trying to force Pershing to see the war his way. When Pershing suggested that the Americans had enough men to participate in both the St. Mihiel Offensive and a Meuse-Argonne offensive, Foch agreed and promised to keep the American army together. He then went one step further, placing all supporting French troops for the St. Mihiel operation under Pershing's overall command. Instead of Americans under French control, French soldiers would be under American control. Foch also placed all Allied aircraft under American control. With one brilliant stroke of diplomacy, Foch averted a crisis with his American allies and saved the critical St. Mihiel Offensive.

Once again time was of the essence. Ludendorff, seeing the threat, began to evacuate the St. Mihiel salient on September 8. A combined Allied air force of 1,481 planes, including French, American, Italian, and Portuguese aircraft, led the assault. It was the largest concentration of airpower in the entire war. Allied infantry moved quickly into the salient, partly because of the effect of the airpower and partly because the Germans had already moved several units to the rear. Within just four days, a salient that had threatened Champagne throughout the entire war had been eliminated. The Allies captured 13,000 prisoners and more than 460 heavy guns at a cost of fewer than 7,000 total casualties.

Foch demanded that the Allies not let up, despite having lost almost 500,000 men since July. He directed Pershing to begin an offensive at the Meuse-Argonne on September 26, just ten days after the end of the St. Mihiel operations. He also ordered the British to attack the fortified German defenses known as the Hindenburg Line. Behind that line sat open country all the way to the Rhine River. British forces broke through the line at several places between September 27 and October 5. At the same time, the Americans continued to advance into the Meuse-Argonne sector, though their progress was much slower than it had been near St. Mihiel. Foch understood that Pershing's offer to conduct both offensives would necessarily mean that he could not expect the Americans to move as quickly as he might have preferred. He was therefore content to allow Pershing to advance at his own pace.

Clemenceau, however, objected both to Pershing's slow progress and Foch's unwillingness to order him to move faster. One of Foch's biographers noted that by early October, Clemenceau had grown fearful of Foch's growing popularity. The prime minister "acquired a fixed idea that Foch was a second Boulanger, threatening civil power."[8] As noted in chapter 1, Clemenceau had read numerous reports that alleged that Foch had antirepublican and proclerical tendencies. Although he had never held these accusations against Foch in the past, Foch had also never held the power and prestige that he possessed in October 1918. Clemenceau's almost pathological distrust of France's military men returned as a change in France's battlefield fortunes turned Foch into a national hero on a par with Napoleon.

On October 11, Clemenceau drafted a letter to Foch that virtually ordered him to take over Pershing's command in the Meuse-Argonne. Clemenceau wrote, "[T]he nation commands you to command."[9] President Poincaré, who held more suspicions about Clemenceau than about Foch, urged Clemenceau to tone the letter down. Ultimately, the prime minister sent a milder version of the letter, but the revised edition nevertheless included a veiled threat at Foch's continued role as generalissimo if he could not force Pershing to move faster. Foch, whose natural inclination was to allow national commanders to command their own units, disregarded the letter, later writing, "I took absolutely no notice of it whatever."[10] In fact, soon after reading the letter, Foch actually extended Pershing's area of responsibility. The incident was an ominous portent of trouble between Clemenceau and Foch.

Despite indications that Germany was preparing to ask for peace terms, Foch planned to continue attacking until the Germans surrendered. His order of the day on October 12 reveals his aggressive thinking. "Germany knows she is beaten and demands peace talks. . . . You will avenge your dead, you will deliver humanity. Soldiers of liberty, forward!"[11] Foch began to plan for an offensive into Lorraine with 28 divisions and 600 tanks. With winter approaching, he feared that the Germans might retreat east of the Rhine River and re-form their armies for new offensives in 1919.

He did not believe that the Germans were ready to consider an armistice in good faith, despite the surrenders of Bulgaria in September, the Ottoman Empire in October, and Austria-Hungary on November 4. Upon learning of the peace note sent to President Wilson by Prince Max of Baden on October 4, he declared it was a "trap" designed to give Germany time to regroup. Foch therefore urged new offensives to push Allied armies across the Rhine River before the onset of winter complicated military operations.[12]

In spite of Foch's fears, Clemenceau formally asked him to advise the government on armistice terms acceptable to the Allied commanders. Foch had little interest in Wilson's Fourteen Points, which he saw as more political posturing. On October 8, Foch responded to Clemenceau's request with three main conditions and six supplementary conditions without which he could not recommend a cease-fire or armistice. The three main conditions were: German evacuation of Belgium, France (understood to include Alsace and Lorraine), and Luxembourg within fifteen days; the creation of three Allied military bridgeheads across the Rhine River; and the imposition of reparations. The supplementary conditions called for Germany to surrender, rather than destroy, railroad stock, industrial resources, and military matériel in the evacuated areas.

Clemenceau became alarmed at the scope of Foch's conditions, many of which he believed were the sole preserve of the civilian government. He flatly denied Foch's request for the Ministry of Foreign Affairs to send a liaison officer to Foch's headquarters, suspecting Foch of trying to influence decisions that were not constitutionally his to make. As he told Lloyd George and Edward House, President Wilson's representative in France, "If Foch decides, the governments are suppressed."[13] Clemenceau was not alone in his concerns. Lloyd George also harbored deep suspicions about the political aspirations of Haig. But in France these suspicions were much more pernicious, wedded as they were to a long and intense history of civil-military discord that had often seemed to threaten the very existence of the Republic itself.

Nor was Foch immune to suspicions of his own. He saw an armistice as a purely military concern, a temporary cessation of military activity within which peace could be discussed. Politicians, he believed, were incompetent to judge the military requirements for an armistice or to negotiate for its terms. As he told Clemenceau, the only men "qualified to deal with the conditions of an armistice are the commanders-in-chief. . . . They alone are thoroughly informed as to the state of their armies and of the enemy forces confronting them."[14] Foch was equally as insensitive as Clemenceau to the delicate balance necessary to maintain political harmony in Third Republic France. He therefore deserves a healthy share of the blame for the decay of French civil-military relations in 1918 and 1919.

Battle lines were thus forming between Foch and Clemenceau that impaired the close cooperation needed between civil and military authority. At such a critical time as October 1918, each man came to see the other as an enemy almost as implacable as the Germans. Foch rejected outright the position of Clemenceau and Foreign Minister Stéphane Pichon that he, as a military leader, should not, as a matter of propriety, and could not, as a matter of law, participate in peace negotiations. Foch wrote:

Peace is the logical finish of a war, and as it was close upon us, I wanted to know the government's policy on the vital question of the Rhine, so as to turn my own steps in the same direction. That was all. As for the notion so vociferously proclaimed by M. Pichon and M. Clemenceau, that a general works on one side of a barrier and the politicians and diplomats on the other, there is nothing more false, or, one can even say, absurd. War is not a dual object, but a unity; so, for that matter, is peace. . . . The two aspects are clearly and inseparably linked.[15]

Foch's firm desire to establish military bridgeheads across the Rhine River quickly emerged as the most contentious issue. At a meeting with all of the national commanders and their staffs on October 25, Foch produced a book that argued that, to invade Germany, one only needed bridgeheads across the Rhine at Cologne, Coblenz, and Mainz. He then turned to the assembled officers and announced that the book's author was Helmuth von Moltke the Elder, the principal architect of Prussia's victory over France in 1870–71. Moltke's words impressed Foch deeply and, with the support of Pétain and Pershing (though not Haig), he soon became obsessed by the question of the bridgeheads. Allied politicians, Clemenceau above all, believed that Foch had no authority in such areas. "Frontiers," Woodrow Wilson said, "have nothing to do with soldiers."[16]

On October 26, Foch clarified his thoughts on the bridgehead issue in a memorandum summarizing the views of the national commanders regarding armistice terms. He demanded bridgeheads with radii of approximately eighteen miles each in the three locations laid out by Moltke. He also reiterated the demand that Germany evacuate all occupied territory without damaging civilian and military equipment contained therein. Pressed by Pétain and Haig to add specifics, Foch also argued that Germany must surrender the following as insurance against their resumption of an offensive: 5,000 heavy guns; 30,000 machine guns; 5,000 locomotives; 150,000 railway cars; and 150 submarines. At British insistence, Foch demanded that the blockade of Germany continue until the conclusion of a final peace treaty.

Foch told President Poincaré that these terms were the minimum armistice terms that the Allied governments could accept. If Germany rejected any part of these terms, he told Poincaré, the Allies should resume the offensive immediately. Still, Foch genuinely hoped and believed that Germany would accept these terms and thereby make further offensives unnecessary. He especially did not want to invade Germany. He told Edward House, "I am not waging war for the sake of waging war. If I obtain through the armistice the conditions that we wish to impose on Germany, I am satisfied. Once this object is attained, nobody has the right to shed one more drop of blood."[17]

On November 7, an Eiffel Tower radio station operator received a message announcing that the German government had selected five plenipotentiaries to discuss armistice terms with Foch personally. Foch told his staff to direct the Germans to an empty forest clearing near the village of Compiègne, but not to give them any clues as to their exact whereabouts. Foch went to Compiègne in a vintage Second Empire railroad car with other Allied military representatives. Consistent with his understanding of an armistice, Foch saw no reason to invite either Poincaré or Clemenceau to accompany him. He also feared that, with peace so close, the involvement of politicians could spoil his best chance to end the war on his terms.

Also consistent with his understanding of the purpose of an armistice, Foch was outraged when he discovered that the German delegation included two civilians. The delegation was also surprisingly low in rank and stature. Foch had to ask for introductions as he did not recognize any of the Germans. He had also noted that Gen. Detlef von Winterfeldt was wearing the French Cross of the Officer of Legion of Honor, bestowed upon him before the war, but revoked on the outbreak of the war. Winterfeldt saluted Foch, expecting a salute in return as a common military courtesy. Instead Foch said sharply, "Monsieur, I authorize you to remove that cross at once from your breast." Winterfeldt "sheepishly" obeyed and the delegations sat down to begin discussions.[18] The Germans, initially taken aback by the harshness of their reception and still unsure exactly where they were, sat bewildered. Foch had designed their reception to remind them at every step who had won the war and who had lost it.

Having thus set the tone, Foch icily asked, "What do you want of me?" The civilian chief of the delegation, Matthias Erzberger, said that they had come to receive proposals regarding an armistice. Foch told him that he had no proposals to make. The Germans, perhaps believing that an error in translation had occurred, told Foch that they had come to receive conditions for the armistice. Foch told them he had no conditions to offer, but he told Erzberger that he could inform him "of the conditions subject to which [an armistice] can be obtained." He then directed Weygand to read the conditions, which were largely those of his October 26 memorandum.[19]

Foch and his staff remained absolutely deaf to the pleas of the Germans. When one member of the delegation complained that maintaining the blockade would risk the lives of thousands of civilians, Foch sharply replied:

> I would remind you that this is a military armistice, that the war is not ended thereby, and that it is directed at preventing your nation from continuing the war. You must also recollect a reply given to us by Bismarck in 1871 when we made a similar request [for leniency] to what you are making now. Bismarck then said "Krieg ist Krieg" and I say to you, la guerre est la guerre.[20]

Foch gave the Germans seventy-two hours to consider the terms, but insisted that they were unalterable and that hostilities would continue until the Germans accepted. He bluntly dismissed the Germans and returned to his private room to telephone Clemenceau.

Peace seemed so close yet so tenuous. Over the next seventy-two hours, many Allied leaders urged Foch to accept lesser terms if Germany gave indications that they would continue to fight. But Foch was determined to conclude an armistice on his terms only. He denied German requests to remove the clauses calling for the Allied bridgeheads and the maintenance of the blockade.

German arguments that they needed a strong army to deal with Bolshevik uprisings also fell on deaf ears, as did requests for extensions in light of the abdication of the Kaiser. Nor were the Germans his only problem. Clemenceau wanted a greater civilian role in the negotiations at Compiègne, but Foch succeeded in keeping him in Paris. He also had to argue against the wishes of Pershing, Poincaré, and Pétain who wanted to invade Germany to make the Allied victory more complete. Foch told the members of the Supreme War Council, "Perhaps another fifty or a hundred thousand Frenchmen would be killed for a moot result. I'd reproach myself for it all my life. Enough blood has flowed. That's enough."[21]

With the Germans he was just as firm, yielding on only the most minor of points and constantly reminding them that the seventy-two-hour discussion period was rapidly expiring. Finally, at 5:18 in the morning of November 11, the Germans signed the armistice. Foch dismissed the delegation without shaking their hands and issued orders for all hostilities to cease at 11:00 the same morning. The war was over. Foch headed immediately to Paris and handed the signed armistice to Clemenceau, telling him, "My work is finished; your work begins."[22] But Foch's work was not done. He had won a war, now he had to win a peace. And in that fight, his main foes would not be Germans but a fellow Frenchman.

Chapter 7

Losing the Peace

WHEN FOCH told Clemenceau, "My work is finished; your work begins," he had acted within all due propriety and respect to alleviate the tensions in French civil-military relations. According to Foch's understanding, the armistice had been a purely military concern. He believed that he had acted legally and followed sound military principles by keeping the civilian government away from the negotiations. According to the French constitution, which placed foreign relations squarely within the offices of the prime minister and the foreign minister, Foch's work was indeed over. In turning the peace treaty over to Clemenceau, he placed foreign affairs within the proper purview of the civilian government.

Despite the smooth conclusion of the armistice, however, Foch continued to harbor doubts. The Germans had signed the armistice, but had remained defiant, stating, "A nation of seventy millions suffers but does not die." Nor did German militarism abate in Foch's eyes, as the German army received a hero's welcome when it marched into Berlin. Foch had little faith that the Germans, believing as they did that their armies had not been defeated in the field, would abide by the conditions agreed to at Compiègne. They had quickly pleaded with the Allied governments to amend some of the conditions of the armistice to help them put down Bolshevik uprisings inside Germany. Foch saw in their pleading a perfidious scheme to avoid or amend the terms to which they had agreed. "With the Germans," he declared, "one must be prepared for anything."[1] He saw Germany as a mortal enemy that would continue to pose a serious threat to France.

Foch harbored suspicions about Allied politicians as well. Above all, he believed that they did not sufficiently understand military issues. He saw Woodrow Wilson's Fourteen Points as only the beginning of a solution toward neutralizing German militarism, and a naïve one at that. He placed no faith in the proposed League of Nations, calling it mere "Geneva chit-chat." He saw the League as an organization comprising politicians, most of whom had no real insight into European security concerns. The proposed borders of Eastern Europe, for example, seemed to Foch impossible to defend. Presciently, he argued that those borders would be susceptible to future German invasions.[2] Permanent disarmament, he repeatedly warned, would not work either because of the difficulties inherent in enforcement. "We can no more limit the number of men trained to arms in Germany," he cautioned, "than the Germans could limit the output of coal in England."[3] He foresaw that even if the Allies could impose numerical limits on the German army, the Germans would still be in a position to create a small, highly trained army that could be easily expanded at some future date.

He placed scarcely more faith in early discussions about a military alliance among the United States, Great Britain, Belgium, and France. Having experienced firsthand how difficult it was to manage a wartime coalition that had held together only out of dire necessity, he recognized that the Allies would not be able to maintain an effective alliance in peacetime. He expected the Americans to return across the Atlantic at the first opportunity and then demobilize. He also believed that Great Britain would vacate the continent, return to a policy of "checking the victor," and press for a balance of power on the continent.[4] Such a balance of power would require France to cede many of the advantages for which it had fought so hard and suffered so much. Even if a military alliance could be arranged, he argued, it would take the British one year, and the Americans two years, to deploy effective fighting forces on the continent. With the advances in mechanization of ground forces since 1914, Foch believed that one year, let alone two, would be far too late to save France from an aggressive and determined neighbor.

Foch had quickly grasped that despite its recent victory, France's postwar condition was not as advantageous as it seemed. The great Russian counterweight, so critical to diplomatic and military planning in the prewar years, was now gone. After 1917, an alliance between the Western Powers and Bolshevik Russia was out of the question. Furthermore, French industry lay in shambles, partly as a result of the normal destruction of war and partly as a result of an intentional German policy that destroyed French industrial works in areas they vacated. Germany's industry, on the other hand, remained almost completely intact. Most ominously, France (including Alsace and Lorraine), Belgium, and Luxembourg together had 45 million inhabitants against as many as 75 million in Germany and Austria.

Foch firmly believed, therefore, that the Allies had to establish the Rhine River as Germany's western boundary. They also had to maintain their three bridgeheads on the right bank of that river. In a note to Clemenceau written on November 26, 1918, Foch contended that, "without this fundamental precaution Western Europe would still be deprived of all natural frontiers, and it would lie open to the dangers of an invasion."[5] Foch had not been willing to step away from the peace negotiations solely out of deference to French constitutional principles. More important, he had stepped away from the peace process because he believed that Clemenceau shared the goal of either detaching the Rhineland from Germany or committing to a French military occupation of the region.

The idea of creating a separate Rhenish Republic had wide support in all French political parties, except the socialists, who were divided over the issue. From 1915 to the end of the war, several books appeared that argued that the Rhineland, like Alsace and Lorraine, was neither ethnically nor culturally German. Other books argued that the region's true roots were Gallic, thus explaining, among other traits, its affinity for wine production. These arguments fit with President Wilson's demand for national self-determination. If the Rhineland were not truly German, these writers argued, then the president's own ideology suggested that it could not properly be permitted to remain inside a German nation.

Other Frenchmen promoted the idea of the Rhine River as one of France's "natural frontiers." This position had a long history in France. Louis XIV had believed that the Rhine River was France's proper eastern border. No less an authority than Napoleon himself had declared, "The boundary of the Rhine, like the Alps and the Pyrenees, is a decree of God." Revolutionary heroes like Danton, Carnot, and Siéyès had all agreed.[6] By this self-serving logic, France would not be annexing the region as some socialists alleged, but merely returning it to its rightful place. This position also had strong support from French industrialists, who saw a chance to pull the Rhineland's extensive economic resources away from Germany and toward France, thus helping to rebuild France's shattered economic infrastructure.

Foch's own opinions were a mixture of these viewpoints. He was opposed to outright French annexation of the Rhineland because he understood that the Rhenish peoples, unlike the Alsatians, were essentially different from the French. He believed that the Rhine River was the proper western border of Germany, not the proper eastern border of France. By separating the Rhineland from Germany, he argued, the Allies could save the region from the dominance of Prussia. By reorienting its economy toward France, the Rhineland could prosper economically. Most critically, Foch argued that the Rhineland buffer was necessary to delay any future German attacks on France.

Foch presented a plan for the Rhineland's future at a meeting with Clemenceau, Lloyd George, and Italian Prime Minister Vittorio Orlando in London in December 1918. Foch proposed that a separate Rhenish Republic be created and brought into a military alliance including France, Belgium, Luxembourg, the United States, and Great Britain. Troops from all the alliance nations would guard the Rhine River bridgeheads. To make the idea more attractive to Rhinelanders, he proposed that the new state be exempt from war reparations. This plan overlapped the French Parliament's recommendation that the Rhineland be demilitarized, with the Allies maintaining a military presence on the river itself and in the bridgeheads.

Lloyd George immediately objected. He told Foch that a war-weary Great Britain would not maintain the twenty divisions on the continent that the marshal had proposed. As Foch had expected, the British were apprehensive about France becoming too powerful on the postwar continent. Haig agreed with Lloyd George, stating that he did not wish to contribute British forces to "the creation of a new French European empire."[7] Lloyd George undoubtedly was also thinking of the rivalry emerging with France over the future of Ottoman possessions in the Middle East, an issue that Foch saw as much less important than issues of continental security.[8] Most important, the British prime minister saw in Foch's scheme an Alsace-Lorraine in reverse. In separating the Rhineland, he argued, the Allies would give Germany an instant focus for revenge. Lloyd George recalled the statue representing the city of Strasbourg on Paris's Place de la Concorde, which since 1871 had been wrapped in a black shroud. "Do not allow Germany to erect such a statue," he warned.[9]

Lloyd George's objections did not surprise Foch, but the willingness of Clemenceau to treat the Rhineland issue as a bargaining chip did. Clemenceau, wily politician that he was, realized that he had no chance to gain a separate Rhenish Republic against the strident opposition of Lloyd George. The Americans learned of the meeting and Woodrow Wilson immediately

objected both to the terms of Foch's proposal and its presenta-
tion at a meeting about which the Americans were not informed.
The President was not convinced by the nationalist arguments
of Frenchmen who supported Rhenish separation nor did he see
the Rhineland as essential to French security. Clemenceau therefore tried to gain some advantage from this losing situation by
yielding to Allied wishes on the subject in exchange for guaran-
tees of a military alliance. Such political bargaining disgusted
Foch, who saw the Rhineland issue as absolutely above and beyond negotiation.

With his focus on the Rhineland, Foch was much less con-
cerned with other aspects of the peace negotiations. The Council of Four (Clemenceau, Lloyd George, Wilson, and Orlando)
continually expressed concerns to Foch about the spread of Bolshevism. Foch, for his part, believed that Bolshevism was a dis-
ease that only took root in societies that were sick or
convalescing. He believed that with a general European recovery,
Bolshevism would die of its own accord. He nevertheless prepared grandiose plans at the Council's request for military operations in Russia and Eastern Europe. These plans appear to have
been designed more for the Council's consumption than for any
serious military implementation. The wide range and scope of
the plans carried the message that the Allies needed to maintain
a strong military presence and avoid domestic pressures to demobilize its armies too quickly.

Foch may have also suspected that the Council of Four saw
Eastern European questions as a way to keep the meddlesome
marshal busy drawing up plans that they had no intentions of
implementing. If so, Foch did not fall for the bait and remained
focused on the Rhineland. When asked to go to Poland, Foch
suggested that his personal presence was not necessary and that
Weygand should go in his place. Eastern European issues receive
only a fraction of the attention in Foch's memoirs that he de-
votes to Rhenish questions because Foch viewed Bolshevism and
Eastern Europe exclusively through the prism of French national
security. He was therefore a firm supporter of a strong, inde-

pendent Poland in the hopes that it could serve as a bulwark against Germany. In January 1919, he authorized the release and transfer of Polish units serving in France so that those units could be readied in the event of border disputes with Germany. Poland rewarded his support to their nation by making him a Marshal of Poland in 1923.

For Foch, Alsace, Lorraine, and the Rhineland were all that mattered. On November 25, 1918, Foch achieved his lifetime aim and entered Metz as its conquering hero. "To see French troops marching past the city hall in Metz," Foch said, "was ample reward for all my efforts."[10] He also attended a mass at the city's cathedral, fulfilling a promise he had made to himself forty-eight years earlier. The next day, another adoring crowd greeted him in a newly liberated Strasbourg. After attending ceremonies there, he went on to plan the occupation of the Rhine River bridgeheads, an operation to which he wanted to devote forty infantry divisions and five cavalry divisions from the United States, Great Britain, France, and Belgium.

Still, these triumphs could not overshadow Foch's sense that the politicians were gambling away the Rhineland, the one guarantee of France's future security. Allied politicians had politely listened to his proposal in London, then dismissed it. Worse, they seemed to be marginalizing him personally as the peace process began. After hearing Foch's proposal, Lloyd George remarked, "I admire and love Marshal Foch very much, but on political questions he is an infant."[11] Shortly afterward, Clemenceau submitted the French list of plenipotentiaries to the Paris Peace Conference. It included an intentional snub to the marshal. Foch's name appeared sixth on the list, but France was to seat just five delegates, leaving Foch without an official voice. Foch concluded that he was being excluded and the Rhineland issue, along with France's future security, shunted aside.

Two powerful forces thus conflicted inside Foch. During his entire career he had remained faithful to the principles of *La Grande Muette*, which forbade French military interference in politics. Nevertheless, he saw the sacrifice of millions of Allied soldiers being squandered by misguided politicians who were blind to France's future security needs. The French delegation did not even extend to him the simple courtesy of keeping him informed of events at the conference. In March 1919, he learned from a third party that Clemenceau had officially withdrawn his support for a separate Rhenish Republic. Instead, Clemenceau was placing France's future security in the promise of an Anglo-American military alliance, an idea that Foch had already dismissed as impractical and unrealistic.

Clemenceau's decision led Foch to break with *La Grande Muette*. When the prime minister asked Foch to support the government's abandonment of its Rhineland demands, Foch replied, "You have decided to change your course of action. I believe that the one we were following was correct. I will stay on it." He began to speak publicly more often, deciding that "discipline is not servility." Foch firmly believed that any peace treaty that did not establish the Rhine River as Germany's western border was a betrayal to the men who had fallen in the war. He also believed that to remain silent and "be content with parades under the Arc de Triomphe" was to abandon his obligations to France. The nation, Foch believed, had to know that he "fought for her until the end, during the peace as during the war."[12]

Foch therefore worked to undermine Clemenceau by seeking Rhenish independence on his own. If the Allied politicians would not support Rhenish independence, then he would present it to them as a fait accompli. In doing so, he had important allies. Two generals close to Foch were in strategic positions in the Rhineland. General Emile Fayolle commanded the army group charged with its occupation. That group contained two armies, one of which was the Tenth Army commanded by Charles Mangin, Foch's trusted subordinate from the Second Battle of the Marne. The other occupation army, the Eighth, was commanded by Augustin Gérard. All three men were supporters of Rhenish independence and began to meddle in Rhenish politics.

While little direct evidence links Foch to Rhenish independence schemes, his close professional and personal links to all three occupation generals makes it highly unlikely that he was blind to their activities. Clemenceau's representative in the Rhineland, Under Secretary of State for War Jules Jeanneney, believed that Foch was quite well informed of the Rhenish schemes and that both Fayolle and Mangin kept him regularly up-to-date. Evidence from Foch's personal notebooks indicate that as late as December 1919 he was aware of the activities of separatist movements in the Rhineland, Bavaria, and Hanover.[13] Certainly, no evidence exists to suggest that Foch ever tried to dissuade his generals. Foch even moved his headquarters to the Rhenish city of Kreuznach, presumably to be closer to Fayolle, Mangin, and Gérard.

Mangin emerged as the leader from the French side, establishing links with several independence-minded Rhenish leaders; most important among them were Dr. Hans Dorten and the mayor of Cologne, Konrad Adenauer. Adenauer, the future German chancellor, soon grew disenchanted with the movement and stepped aside, leaving Dorten as the chief organizer of the separatist forces. Dorten envisioned a Rhenish state that would remain within the German customs union, but control its own foreign policy. He did not want the Rhineland to become a part of France, but he desperately wanted to bring the Rhineland out from under the suzerainty of a Prussian-dominated Germany. Such a scheme appealed greatly to Mangin and Foch, both of whom supported the creation of a separate Rhineland, but did not favor outright French annexation.

While Mangin continued to work with Dorten, Foch asked to be heard by the men deciding Europe's future. He demanded the right to speak both to the Council of Four and to the French Council of Ministers. On March 31, 1919, he was scheduled to address the Council of Four on the issue of communications with the German delegation at Spa. Instead, Foch dedicated his allotted time to a lengthy discussion of the future of the Rhineland. Foch warned the assembled politicians and diplomats that if the Allies agreed to a peace treaty that did not include a separate Rhineland, they would be committing suicide.

He also spoke against the proposed military alliance as a feeble guarantee of future security:

> There is no principle by which a victorious nation can be forced to restore the means of her own security to her enemy. After a free people has paid for her independence by more than a million and a half corpses and unparalleled devastation, no principle in the world can force her to live in perpetual fear of her neighbor, and to have alliances as her sole resource against disaster. No principle can prevail over a nation's right to existence or over the right of France and Belgium to secure independence.[14]

Foch then asked for his speech to be translated, only to hear Clemenceau tell him that a translation was not necessary as he believed that Lloyd George and Wilson (neither of whom was fluent in French) understood his main points. Enraged, Foch twice refused to leave the room when Clemenceau dismissed him. The prime minister, evidently embarrassed at his inability to control one of his generals, leant over to Woodrow Wilson and said, "I don't know what to do, he won't leave." An uneasy silence ensued until British Foreign Secretary Arthur Balfour diplomatically suggested a break for tea. Foch stayed on for tea, despite the obvious cue from Balfour that he was not invited. Eventually, Clemenceau whispered into Foch's ear (no record exists of what he said) and the marshal left the room.

Upon returning home, Foch wrote in his diary:

> Watch out: suspect peace, English peace. . . . We must have a program, a tactic, a will. We find ourselves in the presence of an England that has all it wants for the present: the German colonies and the German fleet. We lack future security because [Britain] is not interested. In the presence of an America which seeks its own peace, we must have what we need. . . . It is on the Rhine and nowhere else that we shall find it.[15]

The incident produced a "mulish obstinacy" in Foch to press for the Rhineland issue and a desire by the Council of Four to keep Foch as far away from deliberations as possible.[16] Clemenceau began to fear that Foch would use the Rhineland issue to force a coup d'état. He flirted with the idea of replacing Foch with the much more pliable Pétain. But Foch was too popular with the French people, and Rhineland independence had too much domestic support for Clemenceau to dismiss him. Moreover, Clemenceau did not want to make any drastic moves before the peace treaty ratification process was completed in the French Parliament. He also knew that to dismiss Foch would greatly jeopardize his own chances to win election as France's president in 1920.

Having thus failed with his demands before the Council of Four, Foch went one step further to outright insubordination. On April 6, Clemenceau asked him to deliver a telegram to the German delegation at Spa communicating to them the preliminary terms of the treaty. Foch refused on the grounds that he did not understand the language in the telegram. Clemenceau accused Foch of failing to obey orders and threatened to replace him with Pétain. Foch agreed to send a reworded version of the telegram if Clemenceau would allow him to address the Council of Ministers to state his objections to the treaty terms then on the table. Clemenceau agreed, but later refused Foch the chance to address the ministers.

Having been rebuffed twice by the politicians, Foch turned to the media. Here he was attacking an Achilles heel of Clemenceau who, as a former journalist, had many enemies in the publishing world. In mid-April, another crisis flared after the publication of two newspaper articles, one in the London *Daily Mail* and the other in the nationalist newspaper *Le Matin*. The latter article appeared anonymously, but Foch's staff later admitted that it had approved the text. The former article directly quoted Foch as prophetically stating:

> Having reached the Rhine, we must stay there. Impress that upon your fellow countrymen. . . . We must have a barrier. . . . Democracies like ours, which are never aggressive, must have strong natural frontiers. Remember, that these seventy millions of Germans will always be a menace to us. . . . They are a people both envious and warlike. . . . What was it that saved the Allies at the beginning of the

war? Russia. Well, on whose side will Russia be in the future? . . .
And next time, remember, the Germans will make no mistake.
They will break through into Northern France and will seize the
Channel ports as a base of operations against England.[17]

Clemenceau was furious. Lloyd George and Wilson also
objected. The British prime minister protested to his French
counterpart that "we must have a general who obeys the government."[18] Clemenceau once again thought of replacing Foch, but
realized the domestic difficulties inherent in doing so. Instead he
summoned Foch and demanded an explanation. Foch at first denied knowledge of the *Le Matin* article, then evasively told
Clemenceau that the staff officer who had proofread the article,
and pushed it past a military censor, was away on assignment and
could not be reached. Clemenceau insisted that Foch could not
act against the Council of Four in the media because to do so
would risk passage of the final peace treaty. Foch, despite his disgust at the treaty negotiations, promised Clemenceau that he
would not grant any more interviews nor would he allow his staff
to do so.

Foch therefore survived his audacious, if foolhardy, challenge
to Clemenceau's authority, but tensions with the prime minister
continued to fester. Clemenceau had twice promised Foch the
opportunity to address the Council of Ministers, but, after his
experiences since March 31, he was understandably reluctant to
honor those pledges. President Poincaré, with whom Foch had
met frequently in March and April, intervened on Foch's behalf
and arranged a meeting of the Council of Ministers on April 25.
Poincaré later admitted that, during this period, the two men
had discussed threatening Clemenceau with a joint resignation if
he did not reintroduce the idea of Rhenish independence.[19]
Foch arrived prepared to present the familiar case for an independent Rhineland, but this time with the support of the president and before a much more sympathetic audience.

Clemenceau, aware of the close links between Foch and Poincaré, began the meeting by warning Foch that he had been invited as a consultant only. Before Foch would be allowed to

speak, he had to agree not to participate in any deliberations. Foch reluctantly concurred but demanded that official minutes of the meeting be kept. Clemenceau refused. Angered, Foch presented his arguments, then waited for questions from the ministers. After only a brief question-and-answer period, Clemenceau abruptly announced a short break to be followed by deliberations by the ministers, from which Foch was to be excluded.

The meeting had been a complete failure for the marshal. Foch left the room with French diplomats André Tardieu and Jules Cambon. Furious at the conduct of the meeting, he and Weygand began to take notes in the hallway. When Cambon asked what he was doing, Foch replied, "One day we will be all called before a high court. France will not understand how a victory of its armies was transformed into a national weakness. I will go with a clean conscience and my papers in order. . . . France will then know how and by whom she was defended and by whom she was abandoned."[20]

Three days later, his old friend Sir Henry Wilson informed him of the Council of Four's plan to phase out occupation of the Rhine River bridgeheads. The occupation at Mainz would last fifteen years, that at Coblenz ten years, and that at Cologne five years. It was the first time that Foch had heard of the plan and he exploded with anger. To his thinking, the Rhineland was all that mattered. Now not only were the politicians withdrawing their support for Rhenish independence, they were also planning to eliminate the bridgeheads before Germany had paid its reparations. An Allied military presence on the right bank of the Rhine River, in Foch's view, would guarantee French security, and it would also guarantee that Germany would pay its reparations, scheduled to be paid over a twenty-year (in some plans, thirty-year) period. If France and the Allies began to evacuate the bridgeheads after five years, they would abandon their most effective means to ensure payment.

These debates became even more urgent because a draft of the treaty was due to be delivered to the Germans on May 7. On May 5, Foch protested that he still had not seen a copy of the draft. He refused to transmit the draft to the Germans until he had another opportunity to address Clemenceau, Wilson, and Lloyd George. The next day he did so, reiterating familiar arguments, but also strongly hinting that he would resign if the Allies did not make changes to the bridgehead schedule. The politicians had anticipated this tactic and told Foch that if he tendered a resignation, they would accept it and replace him with Pétain.

Having gotten nowhere with the politicians, Foch turned back to Dr. Dorten and the Rhenish separatists. Foch, according to one scholar, "lurked mostly off stage, but in this farce he was as much impresario as accessory."[21] There was little time to lose, as the Germans were even then considering their responses to the treaty draft. On May 13, Foch received a full briefing at Mangin's Mainz headquarters. A week later, one group of Rhenish independence supporters declared the existence of a state south of the Moselle River that included the coal-rich Saar region. The protagonists were promptly arrested by German authorities, but General Gérard intervened and secured their release. He also began to formulate plans to use French troops to impose a coup d'état. Foch surely knew about Gérard's activities, but he did nothing to stop them.

Nor did he stop Mangin's support of Dorten's plan to declare the Rhineland independent on May 24 at Coblenz. Dorten had consulted the American authorities in Coblenz in the hopes of gaining their support. Instead, they promptly informed Clemenceau of the plot. Clemenceau determined to put a final stop to his generals' scheming. He ordered all French generals to break their contacts with Rhenish separatists. He also reorganized the French armies of occupation and reassigned Mangin, Fayolle, and Gérard away from the Rhineland. Dorten's scheme was over.

Foch had gone to the brink of insubordination to prevent the passage of a treaty he had opposed. Other portents made the treaty failure seem all the more ominous. He saw in the illegal scuttling of the German fleet at Scapa Flow on June 21 evidence of continued German perfidy. He grew even more enraged when a Berlin mob burned French flags that had been captured in 1870. The flags were supposed to have been returned to France. "They are mocking us," he wrote to his wife. "All of Europe is in a complete mess. Such is the work of Clemenceau."[22]

Foch then chose the only option left to him. Declaring, "This is not peace. It is an armistice for twenty years," he refused to attend the signing ceremony on June 28 in the Hall of Mirrors at Versailles. His chilling prophecy has rung through the years as vindication of his opposition to the treaty. The battlefield victories he had fought so hard to win, he believed, had been squandered by politicians who failed to comprehend the magnitude of their own error. His last years saw him lauded as a great hero, but his profound sadness at the treaty's final terms cast a dark shadow over the remaining decade of his life.

Postscript: Life after Versailles

T HE END of the war and the conclusion of the peace treaty did not improve Foch's opinions of Germany or of Clemenceau. During the war, Foch had generally shunned reporters. His experience with the London *Daily Mail* in April 1919 (see chapter 7) had led to an unpleasant confrontation with Clemenceau during which he had agreed not to talk to the media. Once the signing of the Treaty of Versailles became inevitable, however, he again gave interviews in order to make sure that his voice, silenced throughout the first half of 1919, would be heard. Just weeks before the signing, he gave a prophetic interview in which he predicted the future of Europe: "And next time remember, the Germans will make no mistake. They will break through into northern France and will seize Channel ports as a base of operations against England. . . . The Germans will have no arms for another attack you say? Ho, ho! How do you know? By the time they had got them it would be too late."[1]

In another interview given simultaneously to the New York *Sun* and *Literary Digest* in December 1919 he said of the Germans that "they have no scruples, respect nothing, and have for their religion a doctrine of gross and brutal materialism. They fought for conquest, for loot, in spoils, in territory, and in power." Later in the same interview, he said that the German is "a trained bit of destructive machinery, ready to do the bidding, without question, of his masters."[2]

Believing that the war had done nothing to eradicate German acquisitiveness, Foch urged, without success, that France not demobilize too quickly. The failure of the American Senate to ratify the Treaty of Versailles confirmed Foch's mistrust of the proposed military alliance with the United States and Great Britain in which Clemenceau had placed so much faith. In 1921, labor unrest in Britain led Henry Wilson to ask Foch for the release of British troops from the Rhine bridgeheads. Foch had no choice but to accede to his friend's request, but the decision left France alone to guard the bridgeheads. As Foch had predicted, the military alliance that Clemenceau had accepted in lieu of a separate Rhineland had been utterly futile and ineffective, lasting fewer than two years.

In 1921, Foch made his first visit to the United States. As a guest of the American Legion, Foch greeted enthusiastic crowds in fifteen American cities from Boston to Los Angeles. He addressed a crowd estimated in the hundreds of thousands in New York City, accepted eighteen honorary degrees, and reviewed troops at the U.S. Military Academy at West Point and the U.S. Naval Academy at Annapolis. The trip was a great achievement for Foch, although Prohibition meant that he had to make the two-month voyage without a single drop of wine.

While he was in New York, his rivalry with Clemenceau resurfaced. Clemenceau had recently lost an election to succeed Raymond Poincaré as President of France. After his defeat to a relative unknown in French political circles, Clemenceau was preparing a trip to the United States, where as a young journalist he had covered the end of the American Civil War. Foch told an interviewer from the New York *Tribune* that Clemenceau had been politically humiliated in Europe and therefore was coming to America hoping to find an audience that would cheer him.

He referred to Clemenceau as an "old dotard" who had thrown away Europe's best chance for a lasting peace.

Foch remained on active duty until 1923, but, rather than enjoying the fruits of victory, his final months in office were filled with misfortune and gloom. In May 1922 Germany and Russia signed a pact at Genoa. Exact details were unknown at the time, but the pact worried Foch, all the more so because Italy had been involved in the negotiations as well. He thus feared that a German-Russian-Italian diplomatic understanding, or, worse still, a military alliance, was under discussion. France was, of course, the most obvious target of such an alliance. Moreover, the agreement contained trade terms that promised to boost the German economy. With Germany already believed to be in willful default on reparations payments, the pact meant that France would not see any of the newfound German money.

The following month he suffered a personal tragedy when Henry Wilson, then an anti–Home Rule Member of Parliament, was assassinated on the front steps of his house by Irish separatists. Foch rushed to London to be with Lady Wilson, whom he escorted out of the cathedral after the funeral. The assassination saddened Foch deeply and served as a grim reminder that, victory in 1918 notwithstanding, the world remained a dangerous place. In the next seven years, he attended the funerals of many more former colleagues, including Mangin, Haig, and Fayolle.

Shortly after Wilson's assassination, a new crisis emerged. The French government formally accused Germany of being in voluntary default over the issue of reparations. The government advised Foch to prepare the French army for a march on Berlin. Foch warned the government that he could not do so because of the rapid French demobilization and the withdrawal of American and British troops from the Rhineland. A similar incident occurred in 1923 when Germany failed to deliver promised coal shipments. Foch's belief that the French Army was too weak to enforce treaty terms on its own led to a severe crisis in confidence in the treaty itself. Great Britain, for its part, was unwilling to return soldiers to the continent to support the French.

Unable to enforce the terms of the treaty, the Allies turned to what Foch termed a strategy of "grand illusion." He placed absolutely no faith in the Locarno Pact of 1925, which permitted German entry into the League of Nations despite revelations of Germany's illegal fortification of its frontier with Poland. The pact also restored diplomatic legitimacy to France's former foe. Foch was horrified and frightened by recent events. He believed that France's situation by 1926 was in fact weaker than it had been in 1914. As he told the French government that year, "France has neither the army, nor the reserves, nor the provisions, nor the allies, nor the finances of that [pre–World War I] period."[3]

He was even more aghast at the idealism of the Kellogg-Briand Pact of 1928 in which sixty nations agreed to declare war illegal as a state instrument. "Distrust romanticism," he wrote. "It is a form of easy explanation. . . . It only sees enthusiasm and admiration. It ignores analysis."[4] In place of a firm Rhineland guarantee, the Allies had instead allowed Germany, which had already twice been found to be in blatant violation of treaty terms, to enter the League of Nations.

Despite his disgust at the events of the immediate postwar period, Foch followed his lifelong pattern of avoiding politics. He refused several opportunities to seek public office, continuing to look upon politicians as men of words, not action. It is unlikely that he would have enjoyed a career in politics, a field that involves much more compromise than he was willing to undertake. On a state visit to London, he summed up his views on politics thus: "Here we continue to spend a lot of time doing nothing except eating."[5] He rejected the pleas of conservatives that he run for the French presidency in 1920, even though he would have had the chance to defeat Clemenceau in the process. He turned down offers of senate seats from the départements of Finistère (his home district in Brittany) and Moselle (which includes Metz). He also rejected out of hand an overture from the right-wing group Action Française to become their public spokesman.

EUROPE 1924

New Nations

SWEDEN

FINLAND

Helsinki

Revel

ESTONIA

LATVIA

Riga

LITHUANIA

Kaunas

SOVIET
UNION

Moscow

NORWAY

IRISH
FREE
STATE

GREAT
BRITAIN

Dublin

NETH.

London

BELG.

Danzig

East
Prussia

Berlin

Warsaw

GERMANY

POLAND

Prague

Rhineland

CZECHOSLOVAKIA

Paris

Vienna

Budapest

Alsace-
Lorraine

SWITZ.

AUSTRIA

HUNGARY

RUMANIA

FRANCE

ITALY

Belgrade

YUGOSLAVIA

Bucharest

BULGARIA

PORT.

Rome

Sofia

ALBANIA

Ankara

SPAIN

GREECE

TURKEY

Athens

He did, however, accept a seat at the prestigious Académie Française. Though he did not ask to be considered a candidate, he was nonetheless elected unanimously. It was an honor that must have appealed to the old professor in him, even if the distinction must have been tempered by Clemenceau's election the same day. Partly out of a desire not to cross paths with his old nemesis, he spent little time at the Académie, preferring to work in more military surroundings. Writing from a small office in Les Invalides, he completed his memoirs, an account of his actions at the two battles of the Marne, and an elegy to Napoleon. He publicly presented the elegy in the form of a keynote address in front of Napoleon's tomb on the 100TH anniversary of the emperor's death. He was planning to work on an elegy dedicated to another great military hero of France, Joan of Arc, when he contracted pneumonia. He died of complications on March 20, 1929.

But even in death, Foch still insisted on having his voice heard. The marshal had one last surprise for his old nemesis Georges Clemenceau. In the last two years of his life, Foch had arranged for a series of interviews with an old friend, Raymond Récouly. Récouly published the interviews as a book shortly after Foch's death. In the spring of 1929, *Le Mémorial de Foch* (published in English as *My Conversations with the Marshal*) appeared, complete with Foch's unvarnished opinion of the "vain" and "childish" Clemenceau. Foch compared Clemenceau to Don Quixote, tilting at modern-day windmills like the failed Anglo-American military alliance. France, Foch told Récouly, was a rich land being ruined by its own government.[6]

In contrast to the professional tone of Foch's memoirs, the *Mémorial* pulled no punches. Foch outlined all of the mistakes that he believed the "domineering and dictatorial" Clemenceau had made during the process of creating the "hateful" Treaty of Versailles. Foch blamed Clemenceau's personal and professional failures for the passage of a treaty that "cannot fail one day to have the worst results."[7] Clemenceau was not the kind of man to take such insults lightly. Enraged, the eighty-eight year old Clemenceau worked furiously on his own memoirs, *The*

Grandeur and Misery of Victory, completing the book just before his own death in September. The rivalry between the two men thus continued after both their deaths.

Foch's death produced an outpouring of grief and gratitude from an adoring France. More than 400,000 people filed past his casket as it lay in state under the Arc de Triomphe. The casket was then carried to Les Invalides, where it was placed alongside those of France's greatest military heroes.

Foch was fond of saying that if France were ever in trouble, it should call upon Weygand. Foch's defenders have claimed ever since that if France had listened to Foch in 1919, it would not have had to follow his advice in 1940 when Weygand was recalled from Syria in a futile attempt to rescue the nation from another German invasion. By then it was too late to save France from a nightmare that not even Foch could have imagined.

Notes

Preface
1. Joseph Monteilhet, *Les Institutions Militaires de la France* (Paris: Alcan, 1926), 262.
2. Tasker Bliss, "Foch," *Foreign Affairs* 7 (July 1929): 542.

Chapter 1
1. Jean Autin, *Foch* (Paris: Perrin, 1987), 68.
2. B. H. Liddell Hart, *Foch: The Man of Orléans* (Boston: Little, Brown, 1932), 33.
3. Autin, *Foch*, 61–64.
4. Liddell Hart, *Foch*, 41.
5. George Aston, *The Biography of the Late Marshal Foch* (New York: Macmillan, 1932), 117.
6. Joseph Joffre, *The Personal Memoirs of Joffre* (New York: Harper and Brothers, 1932), 12.

Chapter 2
1. Jean Autin, *Foch* (Paris: Perrin, 1987), 122.
2. Hew Strachan, *The First World War: Volume One, To Arms* (Oxford: Oxford University Press, 2001), 224.

3. Joseph Joffre, *The Personal Memoirs of Joffre* (New York: Harper and Brothers, 1932), 268, 295.

4. Frédéric Guelton, "Foch," *14–18: Le Magazine de la Grande Guerre* 8 (Juin/Juillet 2002): 45.

5. Ferdinand Foch, *The Memoirs of Marshal Foch* (Garden City, N.Y.: Doubleday, 1931), 65.

6. Raymond Récouly, *My Conversations with the Marshal* (New York: Doubleday, 1929), 293.

7. Maxime Weygand, *Foch* (Paris: Flammarion, 1947), 115.

8. Martin Gilbert, *The First World War: A Complete History* (New York: Henry Holt, 1994), 70.

9. B. H. Liddell Hart, *Foch: The Man of Orléans* (Boston: Little, Brown, 1932), 112.

10. Autin, *Foch*, 141.

11. Strachan, *To Arms*, 280.

12. Joffre, *Memoirs*, 373.

13. Foch, *Memoirs*, lv–lvi.

14. Liddell Hart, *Foch*, 122.

15. Liddell Hart, *Foch*, 121.

Chapter 3

1. George Aston, *The Biography of the Late Marshal Foch* (New York: Macmillan, 1932), 148.

2. Ferdinand Foch, *The Memoirs of Marshal Foch* (Garden City, N.Y.: Doubleday, 1931), 185.

3. Jean Autin, *Foch* (Paris: Perrin, 1987), 145.

4. Winston Churchill, *The World Crisis*, vol. 2 (New York: Scribner's, 1931), 425.

5. Aston, *Biography*, 180.

6. "General Foch: The Man of Ypres," *Times* (London), February 18, 1915, 9f.

7. B. H. Liddell Hart, *Foch: The Man of Orléans* (Boston: Little, Brown, 1932), 140.

8. Maxime Weygand, *Foch* (Paris: Flammarion, 1947), 93.

9. Autin, *Foch*, 155.

10. Foch, *Memoirs*, 191.

11. Liddell Hart, *Foch*, 173.

12. Liddell Hart, *Foch*, 185.

Chapter 4

1. Ferdinand Foch, *The Memoirs of Marshal Foch* (Garden City, N.Y.: Doubleday, 1931), 213.
2. Winston Churchill, *The World Crisis*, vol. 3 (New York: Scribner's, 1931), 171.
3. Jean Autin, *Foch* (Paris: Perrin, 1987), 179.
4. Autin, *Foch*, 183.
5. Maxime Weygand, *Foch* (Paris: Flammarion, 1947), 138.
6. George Aston, *The Biography of the Late Marshal Foch* (New York: Macmillan, 1932), 240.
7. "General Foch and Age Limit," *Times* (London), October 2, 1916, 8c.
8. B. H. Liddell Hart, *Foch: The Man of Orléans* (Boston: Little, Brown, 1932), 232.
9. Aston, *Biography*, 242.

Chapter 5

1. B. H. Liddell Hart, *Foch: The Man of Orléans* (Boston: Little, Brown, 1932), 258.
2. Liddell Hart, *Foch*, 261.
3. David Watson, *Georges Clemenceau: A Political Biography* (New York: David McKay, 1974), 303.
4. Liddell Hart, *Foch*, 274.
5. Ferdinand Foch, *The Two Battles of the Marne* (New York: Cosmopolitan Books, 1927), 160.
6. Liddell Hart, *Foch*, 275.
7. Maxime Weygand, *Foch* (Paris: Flammarion, 1947), 181.
8. Liddell Hart, *Foch*, 278.
9. Liddell Hart, *Foch*, 278.
10. Liddell Hart, *Foch*, 279.
11. John S. D. Eisenhower and Joanne Thompson Eisenhower, *Yanks: The Epic Story of the American Army in World War I* (New York: Free Press, 2001), 114.
12. Jean Autin, *Foch* (Paris: Perrin, 1987), 234.
13. Liddell Hart, *Foch*, 311.
14. Liddell Hart, *Foch*, 290.
15. André de Maricourt, "Marshal Foch: An Intimate Portrait," *Harpers* 139 (October, 1919): 653.

16. Watson, *Georges Clemenceau,* 299n.

17. George Aston, *The Biography of the Late Marshal Foch* (New York: Macmillan, 1932), 342.

18. Edward M. Coffman, *The War to End All Wars: The American Military Experience in World War I* (Lexington: University Press of Kentucky, 1998), 263.

Chapter 6

1. "Fruits of the Second Marne Triumph," *Literary Digest* 58 (August 17, 1918): 7.

2. B. H. Liddell Hart, *Foch: The Man of Orléans* (Boston: Little, Brown, 1932), 338.

3. Liddell Hart, *Foch,* 345.

4. Jean Autin, *Foch* (Paris: Perrin, 1987), 240.

5. Ferdinand Foch, *The Memoirs of Marshal Foch* (Garden City, N.Y.: Doubleday, 1931), 376.

6. Maxime Weygand, *Foch* (Paris: Flammarion, 1947), 249.

7. John S. D. Eisenhower and Joanne Thompson Eisenhower, *Yanks: The Epic Story of the American Army in World War I* (New York: Free Press, 2001), 187.

8. Liddell Hart, *Foch,* 376. See chapter 1 for more on the "Boulanger Affair."

9. Gregor Dallas, *At the Heart of a Tiger: Clemenceau and His World, 1841–1929* (New York: Carroll and Graf, 1993), 545.

10. Liddell Hart, *Foch,* 380.

11. Weygand, *Foch,* 269.

12. Foch, *Memoirs,* 453–455.

13. Liddell Hart, *Foch,* 395.

14. Foch, *Memoirs,* 456.

15. Liddell Hart, *Foch,* 391.

16. George Aston, *The Biography of the Late Marshal Foch* (New York: Macmillan, 1932), 423.

17. Foch, *Memoirs,* 463.

18. "How Marshal Foch Rebuked a Piece of Prussian Impudence," *Literary Digest* 61 (April 12, 1919): 88–90. See also "A German's French Honor," *Times* (London), February 24, 1919, 8e.

19. Gregor Dallas, *1918: War and Peace* (London: John Murray, 2000), 115.

20. Stanley Weintraub, *A Stillness Heard Round the World: The End of the Great War, November, 1918* (New York: Truman Talley Books, 1985), 156.
21. Autin, *Foch*, 265.
22. Liddell Hart, *Foch*, 405.

Chapter 7

1. B. H. Liddell Hart, *Foch: The Man of Orléans* (Boston: Little, Brown, 1932), 403.
2. Raymond Récouly, *My Conversations with the Marshal* (New York: Doubleday 1929), 291, 270.
3. Liddell Hart, *Foch*, 412.
4. Liddell Hart, *Foch*, 416.
5. Jere Clemens King, *Foch versus Clemenceau: France and German Dismemberment, 1918–1919* (Cambridge: Harvard University Press, 1960), 16.
6. King, *Foch versus Clemenceau*, 4.
7. Gregor Dallas, *At the Heart of a Tiger: Clemenceau and His World, 1841–1929* (New York: Carroll and Graf, 1993), 550.
8. For more on Franco-British rivalry in the Middle East, see David Fromkin, *A Peace to End All Peace: The Fall of the Ottoman Empire and the Creation of the Modern Middle East* (New York: Henry Holt, 1989).
9. King, *Foch versus Clemenceau*, 24.
10. Liddell Hart, *Foch*, 409.
11. King, *Foch versus Clemenceau*, 26.
12. Maxime Weygand, *Foch* (Paris: Flammarion, 1947), 292–293.
13. See Keith Nelson, *Victors Divided: America and the Allies in Germany, 1918–1923* (Berkeley: University of California Press, 1975), 306, 324.
14. Liddell Hart, *Foch*, 418.
15. Weygand, *Foch*, 296.
16. King, *Foch versus Clemenceau*, 51.
17. King, *Foch versus Clemenceau*, 57–58.
18. King, *Foch versus Clemenceau*, 58.
19. See Gordon Wright, *Raymond Poincaré and the French Presidency* (Stanford: Stanford University Press, 1942), 235.
20. Jean Autin, *Foch* (Paris: Perrin, 1987), 285.

21. King, *Foch versus Clemenceau*, 73.
22. Autin, *Foch*, 288.

Postscript

1. "Foch, the Soft-Spoken, Fiery, Scientific, Emotional Marshal of France," *Literary Digest* 61 (June 7, 1919): 68.
2. "Marshal Foch Says What He Thinks of Bolsheviki and Boches," *Literary Digest* 63 (December 20, 1919): 90, 92.
3. Maxime Weygand, *Foch* (Paris: Flammarion, 1947), 348.
4. Jean Autin, *Foch* (Paris: Perrin, 1987), 365.
5. Autin, *Foch*, 325.
6. Raymond Récouly, *My Conversations with the Marshal* (New York: Doubleday 1929), 25, 282.
7. Récouly, *Conversations*, 191, 119, 195.

Bibliographic Note

ALTHOUGH FERDINAND Foch did much to both shape the end of the war and create the role of the multinational commander-in-chief, there is surprisingly little written on him. Always an intensely private man, Foch did not leave extensive diaries. His memoirs, *Memoirs of Marshal Foch* (New York: Doubleday Press, 1931), are selective and give little insight into Foch the man. They are, however, an essential starting point for understanding Foch the commander. Raymond Récouly's *Foch: My Conversations with the Marshal* (New York: Appleton, 1929), provides a closer look, but it depicts an older, bitter man lashing out at his enemies. Because he died so soon after the text was completed, there is some doubt as to how much Récouly may have embellished parts of the work. It is also not clear whether Foch ever had the opportunity to see the manuscript in its entirety.

Récouly is also the author of one of the first biographies of Foch. The title, *Foch: The Winner of the War* (New York: Scribner's, 1920), gives away much of the author's unabashed admiration for Foch. Récouly praises Foch's calm confidence for inspiring his men and preparing them for a decisive charge on the third day of the first battle of the Marne. That victory, he argues, set the tone both for Foch's role in the war and for eventual Allied victory. Overall, Récouly is entirely too positive, but his book is an important work because it was written by a man whom knew Foch well. Maxime Weygand's *Foch* (Paris: Flammarion, 1947) is important for the same reasons, though the author's bias must be taken into account. One must also consider the fact that Weygand was writing at the end of World War II, when a lionization of France's great military heroes seemed critical.

More recently, Jean Autin's *Foch, ou le Triomphe de la Volonté* (Paris: Perrin, 1987), reflects Récouly and Weygand's admiration. Autin praises Foch for being the nation's greatest military mind since Napoleon and fully worthy of comparisons to the Emperor. The book is critical of Clemenceau and postwar French politicians for not heeding Foch's warnings regarding the postwar peace. Available only in French, Autin's work makes use of some Foch family papers and presents some new anecdotes, but it is an uncritical hagiographic work that must be read with some care.

James Marshall-Cornwall, *Foch as Military Commander* (New York: Crane, Russak, and Company, 1972), by contrast, is one of Foch's most strident critics. He describes Foch's understanding of war in 1914 as archaic and erroneous (a charge that Foch would have agreed with). He blames Foch for needlessly adhering to the offensive at the First Battle of the Marne, causing unnecessarily high French casualties. In Marshall-Cornwall's view, Foch continued to apply outdated offensive tactics until well into the 1916 campaigns. Nevertheless, he admired Foch's coordination of Allied armies during the Yser and First and Second Ypres Campaigns, as well as his performance as generalissimo in 1918.

B. H. Liddell Hart's *Foch, the Man of Orléans* (Boston: Little, Brown, 1932) is both a reasonably well-balanced biography and a platform for Liddell Hart's general arguments in favor of the indirect approach and technological solutions to stalemate. Liddell Hart is critical of Foch for adhering too long to frontal offensives and for ignoring the potential of mechanization and airpower. Still, he praises Foch's calm handling of the crisis of 1918. George Aston's *Biography of the Late Marshal Foch* (New York: Macmillan, 1932), is similar in many respects, though he better places Foch's aggressiveness into the context of the Franco-Prussian War and French military ideology between the wars.

In general, the French works on Foch are full of praise, while the British are more critical. The most important American work that deals with Foch at length is David Trask's *The AEF and Coalition Warmaking, 1917–1918* (Lawrence, Kan.: University Press of Kansas, 1993). Trask is primarily interested in General Pershing and the AEF, but he praises Foch for smoothly and deftly handling the integration of the American forces into the overall Allied war effort.

Foch's postwar life receives little attention as well. Jere Clemens King's brief book, *Foch versus Clemenceau: France and German Dismemberment, 1918–1919* (Cambridge: Harvard University Press, 1960), argues that Foch named himself France's peacemaker and advocated terms that were too harsh even for France's vengeful prime minister. Foch, King argues, greatly overstepped his role as adviser and created problems in French civil-military relations. Anyone interested in primary sources on Marshal Foch should consult the Bibliothèque Nationale in Paris and the Service Historique de l'Armée de Terre in the Château de Vincennes.

Index

About the Author

Michael S. Neiberg is professor of history at the United States Air Force Academy, where he specializes in World War I and the relationship of warfare to European and American society. He received his B.A. from the University of Michigan and his M.A. and Ph.D. from Carnegie Mellon University. Professor Neiberg is the author of *Making Citizen-Soldiers: ROTC and the Ideology of American Military Service, 1916–1980* (Cambridge: Harvard University Press, 2000) and *Warfare in World History* (London: Routledge, 2001). He lives in Colorado Springs, Colorado.